OUR COMPELLING INTERESTS

The Value of Diversity for Democracy
and a Prosperous Society

EDITED BY

Earl Lewis and Nancy Cantor

PRINCETON UNIVERSITY PRESS
Princeton and Oxford

Requests for permission to reproduce material from this work should be sent to Permissions, Princeton University Press

Published by Princeton University Press, 41 William Street, Princeton, New Jersey 08540

In the United Kingdom: Princeton University Press, 6 Oxford Street, Woodstock, Oxfordshire OX20 1TR

press.princeton.edu

ISBN 978-0-691-17048-0

British Library Cataloging-in-Publication Data is available

This book has been composed in Sabon

Printed on acid-free paper. ∞

Printed in the United States of America

10 9 8 7 6 5 4 3 2 1

*Dedicated to our late friend, colleague,
and Advisory Board member
Dr. Clement Alexander Price*

Contents

PART TWO: COMMENTARIES

Acknowledgments

In December 2012, staff at The Andrew W. Mellon Foundation convened a group of legal experts, scholars, academic leaders, and others to talk about the use of race as one of several variables that factored in admission decisions at selective colleges and universities. Since 1978, when the United States Supreme Court ruled in the *Bakke* decision that racial quotas were impermissible but race could be one of several factors used to shape a class, colleges and universities with more freshman applicants than seats have striven to remain lawful and accessible. As recently as 2003, the United States Supreme Court reaffirmed the fundamental understanding that diversity is a compelling state interest and that race could be among the many factors used in admissions in university settings. Although the Court would find its application either acceptable or flawed in cases involving the University of Michigan (*Grutter* and *Gratz*), it once again endorsed the general legal principle.

To the surprise of many, the Court decided to hear a case involving the University of Texas at Austin in 2012. Many in the university community had hoped that the Court's ruling in *Grutter* would serve as a guide for the next generation. Instead, when Texas resident Abigail Fisher asserted that her rights had been violated because of the use of race as a variable, the Supreme Court agreed to hear the case. Prior to the *Grutter* and *Gratz* cases, Texas had adopted a so-called 10 percent plan to address the twin goals of fairness and of racial, gender, and ethnic diversity in its university system. Under the plan, the top 10 percent of all high school students would gain automatic admission to the University of Texas. For those falling outside the top 10 percent, overall academic standing, special talents, demonstrated leadership, and other characteristics enabled the university to round out a freshman class. Fisher's record did not earn her admission, however. She asserted that it was because of the use of race by the university.

The December 2012 conversation at Mellon produced two lines of reasoning. First, there is no settled law on matters of race and opportunity. At the time of this writing, we await the Court's decision in the reheard *Fisher* case. Justice Antonin Scalia's death and Justice Elena Kagan's recusal have made predicting the result all the more difficult. Many assume some further narrowing of the application of race as one of the factors in admissions. Others insist that Fisher had multiple pathways for admission to the University of Texas and fell short; moreover, students of color with even better academic profiles than Fisher's also failed to gain admission, so race was not an overly determinative factor.

Whatever the outcome, a second, more salient point emerged during the convening. Too few had an informed understanding of the basic research on diversity and its value to a prosperous democracy. Here diversity means more than race but certainly includes the usage of race. We believe that without the intelligent use of research, decision makers and policy makers retreat to what they believe. Justices may believe that admission into selective colleges harms the self-esteem of students of color, but research by Bowen and Bok in *The Shape of the River* indicates otherwise. Decades of research and new research needs to be showcased to inform current debates. Much of that research has not yet been pulled together and made easily available. The series that this volume inaugurates seeks to fill that void. It is the assembling and accessible presentation of research on diversity that we aim to produce for a broad readership. We want to thank our advisory board members for suggesting potential topics and authors. This collective of scholars, administrators, intellectuals, and researchers continues to improve the products we will deliver. Special acknowledgment is offered of Danielle Allen and Susan Whitlock for their critical reading of the introduction, Madeleine Adams for her deft editorial guidance, and two anonymous readers for helpful questions and suggestions. Makeba Morgan Hill and Doreen Tinajero have tirelessly coordinated advisory board meetings, production schedules, and logistics with authors. Without them, this volume would not have been produced.

A series of this significance could not work without a real partnership. Peter Dougherty, Eric Crahan, and their colleagues at Princeton University Press have proved and continue to prove very able partners. If anything, their understanding of the project and its importance grows with time, as does their enthusiasm.

Finally, we want to thank the Board of Trustees of The Andrew W. Mellon Foundation. The Mellon Foundation has long supported research. This is the first time the Foundation has lent its name to a research undertaking of this scope and duration. The Board's faith in this series is greatly appreciated.

Contributors

DANIELLE ALLEN, Director of the Edmond J. Safra Center for Ethics and Professor of Government and in the Graduate School of Education at Harvard University, is a political theorist who has published broadly in democratic theory, political sociology, and the history of political thought. A 2001 MacArthur Foundation Fellow, she is a member of the American Academy of Arts and Sciences, the American Philosophical Society, and the Society of American Historians.

KWAME ANTHONY APPIAH, Professor of Philosophy and Law at New York University, a noted public intellectual who is currently exploring the connection between theory and practice in moral life, has published widely in African and African American literary and cultural studies. He is a member of the American Academy of Arts and Sciences, the American Philosophical Society, and the American Academy of Arts and Letters.

NANCY CANTOR, noted personality and social psychologist, is chancellor of Rutgers University–Newark. Author of several books, including *Personality Psychology* and *Personality and Social Intelligence*, she was elected to the American Academy of Arts and Sciences and the National Academy of Medicine.

ANTHONY P. CARNEVALE currently serves as Professor and Director of the Georgetown University Center on Education and the Workforce, a position he has held since the Center was created in 2008. Carnevale coauthored the principal affidavit in *Rodriguez v. San Antonia*, a U.S. Supreme Court action to remedy unequal education benefits.

WILLIAM H. FREY is Senior Fellow with the Brookings Institution and Research Professor at the University of Michigan Institute for Social Research. He is author, most recently, of *Diversity Explosion: How New Racial Demographics Are Remaking America.*

PATRICIA GURIN is the Nancy Cantor Distinguished University Professor Emerita of Psychology and Women's Studies, and the Thurnaur Professor, at the University of Michigan. She is a Faculty Associate of the Research Center for Group Dynamics at the Institute for Social Research and of the Center for African and Afro-American Studies.

IRA KATZNELSON has been Ruggles Professor of Political Science and History at Columbia University since 1994, and, since 2012, president of the Social Science Research Council. A fellow of the American Academy of Arts and Sciences and the American Philosophical Society, his most recent book, *Fear Itself: The New Deal and the Origins of Our Time*, focuses on the role of race on American political development.

EARL LEWIS, an American social historian, is president of the Andrew W. Mellon Foundation and a fellow of the American Academy of Arts and Sciences. His several books include *The African American Urban Experience* and *Defending Diversity*.

NICOLE SMITH is the Chief Economist at the Georgetown University Center on Education and the Workforce, where she leads the Center's econometric and methodological work.

THOMAS J. SUGRUE is Professor of Social and Cultural Analysis and History at New York University. A specialist in twentieth-century American politics, urban history, civil rights, and race, he is a Fellow of the American Academy of Arts and Sciences and past president of the Urban History Association and the Social Science History Association.

MARTA TIENDA is Maurice P. During '22 Professor in Demographic Studies, Professor of Sociology and Public Affairs, with joint affiliations in the Office of Population Research and the Woodrow Wilson School at Princeton University. She is a member of the American Academy of Arts and Sciences, the American Academy of Political and Social Sciences, and the National Academy of Education.

OUR COMPELLING INTERESTS

The Value of Diversity for Democracy and a Prosperous Society

Earl Lewis and Nancy Cantor

Stephanie, Cyarah, Sam, Adedoke, Gifty, Ola, Justin, Christian, and Lovanie are a small sample of the students who entered college in the fall of 2015. Their names reflect the currents and cross currents of migration, history, aspirations, and dreams. Some came from families with deep roots in the United States; others proudly proclaimed themselves first generation. In statements composed to introduce themselves to others in their university's social justice learning community, a few made note of their communities of faith, while others paid homage to family and friends who inspired their life choices. In moving prose, they spoke of premature births, early deaths, and personal struggles. Passionately, they talked of what they wanted to become, the dreams they had for themselves, their families, and their communities. Lovanie Pomplilus echoed many of her classmates when she wrote:

> I am the youngest of four children. I am also the only one
> born in America out of all of my siblings. My parents are

from Haiti and they do not speak much English. Throughout my younger years my parents only spoke Creole to me, so when I started school I did not speak or understand English. As a result I took an ESL class, which I enjoyed. After one year of ESL I was able to take regular classes. All my life I had to work really hard in school because I did not receive help at home with my school work.[1]

Like others in her cohort, she imagined a future that she would shape: "I work really hard for the things I want in life, because quitting is never the answer. Although the world we live in makes it easy to fail and hard to become successful, [I] will refuse to let failure consume my life. So I leave you with a quote so dear to me, 'Your future depends on what you do today'—Mahatma Gandhi."[2]

Lovanie's classmate Christian overcame other challenges to find himself among the first-year students. He was quick to remind readers that a person's outside may mask struggles and demons competing for attention internally. Adolescence, regardless of background, can be difficult enough, but in this case, self-loathing, identity struggles, and social alienation certainly exacerbate the movement from child to teenager to adult. He wrote:

Growing up, I struggled with questions of identity. From my picture, you'll see that I'm a light-skinned, red haired, male. I will tell you, however, that I am a Latino queer. As a child, I saw myself as a white, cis-male. Unknowingly, I had engaged in self-negation, and self-hatred. I hated my culture. I hated speaking anything other than English. I hated eating anything other than hotdogs and hamburgers. As I matured, I came to understand my familial heritage, but I continued to struggle with how this implicated the way in which I saw myself. Engaging in critical work, I learned to affirm myself and love those around me, which is an ethos I wish to one day teach along with the aspirations, goals, and dreams of those who fight, relentlessly, for true justice for all.[3]

Christian and Lovanie speak for themselves, but they also exemplify current and future generations of Americans who complicate old notions of diversity and influence how we speak about it. To see them as only black, white, or Latino is to oversimplify how they entered and enter the world. Color, gender, gender identity, and family ties to another land, language, or cuisine mingle with age, race, geography, class, religion, sexuality, and birth order to give form and substance to the lives they are shaping.

Christian and Lovanie attend Rutgers University–Newark, an urban campus populated by students from a wide variety of backgrounds. They applied for college in the age of the Big Test or SAT, an assessment that determines the fates of millions annually. This is an era when educational attainment increasingly sorts people into poverty or relative wealth.[4] Yet their statements reflect the hopefulness of those who have been presented with opportunity. They have come of age at a time dominated by calls to educate more, not less, of our talent pool. They are hopeful, too, about the possibilities for building community out of difference as they progress through pathways of inclusion.

Yet any number of campuses are roiled by the outrage that emerges from experiences of exclusion. In 2015 in university settings as varied as the University of Missouri and Yale, the kinds of campuses often championed as model sites of tolerance and acceptance, students from minority backgrounds frequently called attention to what they experience as individual and institutional examples of hostility, while those who disagree often charge them with hypersensitivity. At Missouri, for example, graduate student Jonathan Butler commenced a hunger strike to force the university to remove the president he deemed unresponsive to a series of racially charged incidents, most notably a feces-constructed swastika in a residence hall bathroom. When asked if he was prepared to die, Butler remarked, "I don't think Tim Wolfe [the president of the University of Missouri] is worth my life. But I do believe that when it comes to fighting for justice, you have to be willing to have a level of sacrifice." Wolfe ultimately resigned after Missouri football players and coaches rallied to the cause. Their protests brought into sharper focus the ways that diversity does not always translate into inclusion.

At Yale, black students blasted administrators of all backgrounds for asking, or at least allowing, students of color to bear a disproportionate responsibility for educating others about demeaning forms of expression, such as ethnically or racially stereotyping Halloween costumes. As in so many moments of protest, students raised other questions: Should a fraternity be allowed to block admission to a party on the basis of race and gender, as was alleged? Why continue to call the heads of the residential colleges *masters*, given the term's usage in American history? Is now the time to close the chapter on the university's allegiance to the nineteenth-century proslavery advocate John C. Calhoun?

The diversification of American life and its institutions can produce positive and negative reactions. Demographers such as William Frey say that Christian and Lovanie will represent an ever-larger share of the American nation in the decades ahead. In fact, the United States is predicted to have a nonwhite majority by midcentury. Demographic transition, some assume, will drive change. The old categories of "minority" and "majority" will evolve, if not disappear, the optimists trumpet. Yet at the same time, and as the foregoing examples suggest, this very heterogeneity has the potential to compromise the ambitions of the American democratic project. As the *New York Times* columnist Frank Bruni described, there is a real worry that heightened difference will exacerbate "sharpening divisions, pronounced tribalism, corrosive polarization."[5]

This inaugural volume in the series Our Compelling Interests: The Value of Diversity for Democracy and a Prosperous Society comes as we contemplate a transforming societal landscape. The series promises to explore diversity—in racial, socioeconomic, gender, religious, regional, sexual, and other forms—through accessible, sophisticated, and balanced treatments by leading scholars, writers, intellectuals, and commentators. The goal is lively, informed analysis, not social or political bromides. We have commissioned studies of how diversity affects social organization and productivity, educational access and testing, crime and incarceration, art and creativity, education and social mobility. Volumes under way ask if diversity improves the bottom line and enhances overall productivity; and if the concept of diversity carries the same meaning in Europe, Asia, Africa, and elsewhere in the Americas.

Aiming to be balanced, informed, and at times edgy and pointed, the series seeks to force even the most ardent skeptic and most devoted proponent of diversity to pause and consider: what are our shared compelling interests as a nation and a civil society? In the law, the idea of "compelling interests" captures those reasons that the state may limit or abridge what are otherwise recognized as protected rights. The state's compelling interest, for instance, in providing equal protection under the law justifies limiting the rights of employers, landlords, and public accommodations in order to achieve nondiscrimination. Yet we might move beyond the legal technicalities to take a more expansive view of the idea of compelling interests. As a society, we share a compelling interest in our constant need to balance the individual's right to escape unwanted state interference against the state's interest in protecting individuals from unfair and unconstitutional treatment. This series seeks to shape this formulation by further asking: Can we ensure a healthy and vibrant democracy without carefully aligning guarantees of civil and human rights, mechanisms for civic connection, and pathways for economic opportunity? Ultimately, we wonder how we advance democracy if we limit the numbers who have reason to believe they have a fruitful stake in its future. Is the perceived legitimacy of American institutions—from those that educate to those that adjudicate, from those that promulgate free expression to those that safeguard our security—at risk when so many are left behind in the "land of opportunity"? For us, issues of fairness and inclusion are themselves a matter of compelling interest.

Accordingly, we ask a number of timely and interlocking questions, beginning with: Is diversity an opportunity for growth or a constraint on prosperity? Is diversity in institutions a goal worth pursuing or a condition to be managed? What happened to our aspirations for finding common cause, despite observable difference, for *e pluribus unum*? Are the hopes of sustaining a prosperous society upended if successive waves of advancement leave scores abandoned and neglected on the shoals?

Efforts to craft broader social and economic inclusion are not new, to be sure. A little more than sixty years ago the country set about dismantling "separate but equal" with the hope of eliminating racially segregated schooling. Just over fifty years ago the nation launched a "War on Poverty" to arrest and correct perceptible inequality. Yet as we pass the half-century mark of this "war," we face escalating, not diminishing, inequality.[6] And six decades after the outlawing of separate but equal, more rather than fewer schools and neighborhoods are segregated, especially in our economically stagnating urban centers.[7] We are left to ask: Have we abandoned our commitment to equal opportunity for all? As the faces, faith traditions, native languages, and social traditions of our neighbors continue to change, gated communities, ever-higher incarceration rates for some youth, and other forms of separation raise the question: Why do we fear the difference in our midst? Could the difference in our midst perhaps rather be the key to our sustained future? The essays in this inaugural volume, as well as the volumes to follow, confront these questions while also probing how we define our shared compelling interests.

Discourse on diversity. A range of studies point to the ongoing demographic transformation of America. By midcentury, Americans living along the Atlantic, Gulf, and Pacific coasts will live amid a notable nonwhite majority, with traditional patterns of sizable white majorities continuing to dominate in the interior Midwest, plains, and mountain West. The nonwhite majority will not constitute a monolith, however. The largest group is projected to be Hispanic, which includes a broad cross section of Spanish speakers—with roots in Puerto Rico, Mexico, Cuba, Guatemala, the Dominican Republic, and elsewhere. African Americans will comprise a second population cluster, remaining 13–14 percent of the overall population. But even here, the population composition will continue to shift, with an increasing share of those, like Lovanie, with roots in a broader African diaspora. Some will hail from the Caribbean and confound the simple interplay between race and ethnicity, being both black and Latino, or black but not multigenerational African American. Others will have grown up with parents in the United States and grandparents on the African continent, members of a contemporary and swelling American African population. A quickly growing Asian-descended population will blend strands from several nations of origin—China, Japan, the Philippines, Korea, India, Vietnam, Thailand, Samoa, Guam, and Pakistan—with long-established communities to give form to the Asian American population.

A focus on percentages alone obscures the continued presence of this country's indigenous peoples and the growing numbers who consider themselves mixed race. We have frozen native peoples in time, substituting one-dimensional Hollywood images for the varied communities that stretch from the Arctic Circle in Barrow, Alaska, to the Gulf Coast in Mississippi. Native Americans live in rural areas and cities, on reservations and in suburbs; they head major enterprises and struggle with human afflictions, and will demand attention in the quarter century ahead.

Alongside them expect to find a greater number of Americans who refuse to answer the question of whether they are white, black, brown, yellow, or red. America's racial chromatic scale has less meaning for them as they embrace the multiple histories that formed them. Old binaries of one race or the other, one language or the other, one religion or the other will mean less to the kid who grew up celebrating Christmas, Hanukkah, and Kwanzaa and whose best friend is Muslim and speaks French fluently. They, too, are part of the change we are to see.

Numbers alone won't trigger a commitment to diversity or recognition of our shared compelling interest in leveraging diversity for democracy and prosperity. As post–World War II South Africa vividly attests, a numerical majority need not always lead to full political and social opportunity. From restrictive voting rules, to prohibitions on membership, to the criminalization of certain behaviors, to overheated, bigoted political rhetoric, to subtle residential steering by real estate agents, societies can draft ingenious tools to prevent diversity from changing the status quo. Clusters of individuals come together to advantage their own group or perspective, failing to ask what's best for the common good.

Attempts to engage aspects of our common interests are numerous and varied. In some ways, we are awash in such conversations in virtually every arena of American life. Often the focus is on obstacles to full participation faced by too many Americans and on the proper role to accord to particular dimensions of difference, especially race, ethnicity, and class in opening up avenues for social mobility, opportunity, and civil rights. These conversations capture our hearts and our minds, whether framed by the courts, by Congress, or by the media; whether focused on school desegregation, access to higher education, immigration reform, voting rights, a cradle-to-prison pipeline, disparities in health and wealth, or global economic competitiveness. They are riveting whether cast in the haunting light of history (Is this a new Jim Crow?),[8] viewed through the hopeful visions of prophets of a postracial, color-blind future,[9] or anchored in the alternative vision of a society enriched by leveraging that diversity and difference.[10] Sometimes these conversations can seem too technically focused on legal claims and arguments of precedent, far from the realities of lived lives. At other times, it is harder and harder even to have the conversation, especially in the light of the frequent clashes that begin with intense intergroup distrust and suspicion and end in tragic confrontation. Certainly, what one group sees as enlightening debate, or even equal-opportunity satire, another sees as targeted provocation in light of what it holds sacred. How, then, do we learn to value the freedom of expression and the responsibility of listening?

Documenting the landscape. This inaugural volume, *Our Compelling Interests: The Value of Diversity for Democracy and a Prosperous Society*, seeks to set the context for the volumes to follow by asking how we reconcile the core national principle of equal opportunity for all with the failures that still haunt our current realities, the divisiveness in our social landscape, and what promises to be more, not less, difference given the demographic explosion we are poised to encounter. In other words, how do we consider the pursuit of civil rights, social connectedness, and prosperity in an age of fragmentation? Will the diversity explosion that William Frey describes in the first essay of this volume lead us to make ever firmer and crisper distinctions of identity, fighting with one another as if forever caught in a zero-sum world, or will we instead mobilize to take the complexity and dynamics of that changing landscape as an opportunity to break out of our historical patterns? Will the world that Christian and Lovanie graduate into soften enough to allow the nuances of their worldviews to lead down a path that leverages difference and opens up opportunity as a shared interest? The answer is by no means clear. Recognition of this is itself an important turning point for our nation, and the world.

Indeed, as all the essays in this volume note, we cannot simply presume progress, especially as patterns of residential, educational, and economic segregation have in many ways hardened over decades. While the demographic map reflects a blurring of canonical groupings, Charles Tilly's "durable inequalities" hold fast.[11] We see widening divides between the "haves" and the "have nots," greater social distrust across lines of difference, sharper instances of education serving the interests of some kids more than others, and other patterns disturbingly aligned with historically familiar group dynamics. These patterns require us to take seriously the relentless drag backward, to segregated neighborhoods, schools, prisons, and workplaces, that Thomas Sugrue compellingly describes here. This in turn sets the table for Danielle Allen to articulate a need for policies and skills of interaction that build social connectedness. The durability of inequality also puts us on notice that, if we fail to educate inclusively, we may well face diminishing prospects for a prosperous society, as highlighted here by Anthony Carnevale and Nicole Smith. This concern leads Marta Tienda to call for policies of human capital investment in the education of youth, especially the burgeoning minority youth cohorts.

Defining diversity. The structural lines that simultaneously define diversity and solidify inequality along familiar divides—of race, ethnicity, class, home, or birthplace—have in some very real way intensified since the civil rights legislation of the 1960s (as Sugrue notes). At the same time, though, the social landscape of diversity, identity, and group affiliation has taken on more complex intersectionality as more people move across national and cultural boundaries, and other critical dimensions of difference—gender, sexuality, ability, faith—gain attention (as Allen notes). Both the intensification of demarcations by race and ethnicity and the complex, more fluid landscape of identity surface here as essential to any discussion of civil rights, social connectedness, and full economic participation. This tension in definition and focus—often characterized, on the one hand, by a concern that the power of race gets lost in an inclusive definition of diversity and, on the other hand, by the need not to overlook other significant dimensions of difference—highlights how much harder the task of leveraging diversity will be in the future and how complex the answers will be.

When Sugrue traces the time line of racialized inequality, and Carnevale and Smith lay out the economic imperative for full educational and workplace participation by the fastest-growing racial, ethnic, and immigrant groups, there is little doubt of the potential value of diversity as defined in traditional terms. This potential value is true, Sugrue points out, even as the normative particulars of racial and ethnic categorical distinctions shift and blur (as they always have). Yet, when the discussion moves in Allen's essay to bridging social ties and the social construction of social connectedness, then the power of broader, more fluid, more inclusive, and yet textured identity categories emerges just as clearly. This is when the lived experiences—the internal psychology and the external interactions that motivate Lovanie and Christian to push onward against traditional binaries—become useful to examine. This contextual specificity is, in our view, inevitable and provides a more comprehensive, albeit also more complicated, picture of diversity—its manifestations and impacts and potential value.

Although Allen is certainly right to warn us against reifying particular salient categories of difference and identity, as they are socially constructed and fluctuate with associational habits and context, life opportunities remain structured by durable inequalities that articulate with race, ethnicity, class, and neighborhood. And those durable inequalities, as Sugrue argues, also determine the salience and longevity of particular group distinctions. In turn, we are led by both Sugrue and Allen, along with the commentaries of Ira Katznelson and Patricia Gurin, to question whether we are on a path of relentlessly increasing isolation (bonding within but not bridging across groups) or on one of increasing connectedness without assimilation. Are there instances in which more demographic diversity—population heterogeneity produced by immigration in some cases and changing patterns of association in others—isn't accompanied by increasing inequality? Will our implicit biases and default assumptions relax enough to allow us to perceive just how complex and multi-identified people have become? Will it help as we move forward to think of diversity in more than demographic terms, as the commentaries of Katznelson and Kwame Anthony Appiah suggest?

In this volume, we start this process of interrogation of our compelling interests in order to find the right way to examine and respond to increasing diversity. We understand the fuller exploration of our compelling interests that marks this series will not be easy. We will need to overcome habits of conflating the concept of diversity with white-black interactions. We appreciate the need to include research that confounds rather than affirms initial assumptions. As the series develops, moreover, we must be poised to reassess what counts as a compelling interest.

Leveraging diversity. To leverage diversity is to use it to promote the common good. This requires us to ask new questions and to reexamine old conclusions. How do we recognize the long arm of pervasive racial binaries and at the same time go beyond descriptions of structural or representational diversity— that is, the number of individuals in specific categories? What will it take to recognize, for example, the very real threats posed by hyper-residential segregation? This "architecture of segregation"[12] hinders our ability to live together, reduces our ability to learn from one another, and often leads to significant differences of opinion. As important, how do we consider the dynamic complexity of diversity? Words such as intersectionality, hybridity, and blurred group demography speak to the ways an individual can occupy many social categories, simultaneously. As the authors and commentators in this volume note, shifting social group composition and norms, and the changing landscape of power, inform what is meant by diversity and how it can be best leveraged.

In fact, it is not just the salient descriptive (or prescriptive) dimensions of diversity that shift in influence over time and context; it is also the ways in which individuals perceive diversity as they interact with each other. Diversity is never enough in and of itself to produce compelling impact, as Gurin and Tienda strongly assert here, and as many educators have noted in valuing the educational benefits of diversity.[13] Proximity is not the same as interaction. We argue that a true democracy depends on individuals from different communities being presented with informed and intentional opportunities to learn from one another. This is true whether the measured result centers on social interaction (as in Allen's essay) or economic productivity (as in Carnevale and Smith's) or intergroup inequality and the distribution of wealth and power (as in Sugrue's). As Appiah wisely notes, whereas unfettered inequality can destroy democracy, embracing diversity can spur creativity, productivity, and prosperity. Attention must be paid to the social and behavioral dynamics of effective inclusion, full participation, and intergroup interaction. An accumulating literature across domains as disparate as education, the behavior of firms, public health, and community policing, underscores this point as does Katznelson in his commentary on democratic diversity. As a result, we take as a "first principle" that making diversity work is a positive societal value.[14] Indeed, for democracy to work, we must leverage the range of human actors who contribute to the overall well-being of our society.

Valuing diversity. We can succeed in defining and leveraging diversity and still fail to value diversity's role in sustaining a prosperous democracy. To value is to signal importance. This volume, and the series it inaugurates, argues that diversity in all forms must be valued. It further suggests that everyone's civil rights must be respected, social connectedness in all aspects of civil society must be encouraged, and participation in the economy should be based on ability and open to all. The interactions among diversity, civil rights, social connectedness, and economic opportunity are key to realizing a fully prosperous society.

Of course we recognize the tension between what is professed and what is experienced. In principle, a society can profess a belief in the value of diversity and in practice limit the benefits of its application (whether through political attacks, legal battles, or social worries) to a small community of participants. This series hopes to influence the continued evolution of conversation and thought about the interplay between diversity and democracy—in the United States and other countries.

In conclusion, for Lovanie and Christian to realize their dreams and play a significant role in shaping their communities, this nation, and our world, diversity must be valued, defined, and leveraged. As is argued in the pages that follow, we have a compelling interest in doing so.

The "Diversity Explosion" Is America's Twenty-first-Century Baby Boom

William H. Frey

America reached an important milestone in 2011.[1] That occurred when, for the first time in the history of the country, more minority babies than white babies were born in a year.[2] Soon most children will be racial minorities—Hispanics, blacks, Asians, and other nonwhite races. And, in about three decades, whites will constitute a minority of all Americans. (See figure 1.) This milestone signals the beginning of a transformation from the mostly white baby boom culture that dominated the nation during the last half of the twentieth century to the more globalized, multiracial country that the United States is becoming.

The sweep of diversity that has just begun to affect the nation became obvious from my examination of the 2010 U.S. census, census projections, and the results of the 2008 and 2012 presidential elections. As a demographer who has followed U.S. population trends for decades, even I was surprised by the sheer scope of this change. This is not just more of the same. I am convinced that the United States is in the midst of a pivotal period ushering in extraordinary shifts in the nation's racial

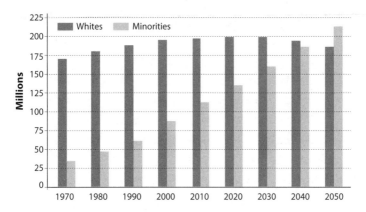

FIGURE 1. U.S. White and Minority Populations, 1970–2050
Source: William H. Frey, *Diversity Explosion: How New Racial Demographics Are Remaking America* (Washington, DC: Brookings Institution Press, 2015).

demographic makeup. If planned for properly, these demographic changes will allow the country to face the future with growth and vitality as it reinvents the classic American melting pot for a new era.

Key among these changes are:

The rapid growth of "new minorities": Hispanics, Asians, and increasingly multiracial populations. During the next forty years, each of these groups is expected to more than double. New minorities have already become the major contributors to U.S. population gains. These new minorities— the products of recent immigration waves as well as the growing U.S.–born generations—contributed to more than three-quarters of the nation's population growth in the past decade. That trend will accelerate in the future.

The sharply diminished growth and rapid aging of America's white population. Due to low white immigration, reduced fertility, and aging, the white population grew at a tepid 1.2 percent in 2000–2010. In roughly ten years, the white population will begin a decline that will continue into the future. This decline will be most prominent among the younger populations. At the same time, the existing white population will age rapidly, as the large baby boom generation advances into seniorhood.

Black economic advances and migration reversals. Now, more than a half century after the civil rights movement began, a recognizable segment of blacks has entered the middle class while simultaneously reversing historic population shifts. The long-standing Great Migration of blacks out of the South has now turned into a wholesale evacuation from the North—to largely prosperous southern locales.[3] Blacks are abandoning cities for the suburbs, and black neighborhood segregation continues to decline. Although too many blacks still suffer the effects of inequality and segregation is far from gone, the economic and residential environments for blacks have improved well beyond the highly discriminatory, ghettoized life that most experienced for much of the twentieth century.

The shift toward a nation where no racial group is the majority. The shift toward "no majority" communities is already taking place as the constellation of racial minorities expands. In 2010, 22 of the nation's 100 largest metropolitan areas were minority white, up from just 14 in 2000 and 5 in 1990. Sometime after 2040, there will be no racial majority in the country. This is hardly the America that large numbers of today's older and middle-aged adults grew up with in their neighborhoods, workplaces, and civic lives. One implication of these shifts will be larger multiracial populations as multiracial marriages become far more commonplace.

The "diversity explosion" the country is now experiencing will bring significant changes in the attitudes of individuals, the practices of institutions, and the nature of American politics. Racial change has never been easy; more often than not, it has been fraught with fear and conflict. Yet for most of the nation's history, nonwhite racial groups have been a small minority. Partly because of that, blacks and other racial minorities were historically subjected to blatant discrimination, whether through Jim Crow laws, the Asian Exclusion Act, or any of the many other measures that denied racial minorities access to jobs, education, housing, financial resources, and basic rights of civic participation.

What will be different going forward is the sheer size of the minority population in the United States. It is arriving "just in time" as the aging white population begins to decline, bringing with it needed manpower and brain power and taking up residence in otherwise stagnating city and suburban housing markets. Although whites are still considered the mainstream in the United States, that perception should eventually shift as more minority members assume positions of responsibility, exert more political clout, exercise their strength as consumers, and demonstrate their value in the labor force. As they become integral to the nation's success, their concerns will be taken seriously.

Yet, change will not come without challenges. In fact, a big part of the impending clashes related to race will have demographic roots because of how diversity spreads across the country—both generationally and geographically.

Diversity by Generation, "From the Bottom Up"

If nothing else, the diversity explosion is generational in character. New minority growth is bubbling up the age structure, from young to old. Today, this growth is most visible among America's children. This has to do, in part, with the more youthful population of Hispanics, the nation's largest minority group. Due to recent waves of Hispanic immigrants who were younger than the total population and to their somewhat higher fertility, Hispanics are decidedly younger than the population at large. This relative youthfulness, with many adults in peak childbearing ages, ensures continued sizable contributions to births, irrespective of future immigration. Asians, the second-largest new minority, also contribute to population gains among youth. In addition, the still tiny multiracial population, with a median age of just around twenty years, has the greatest potential for growth.

Nonetheless, the aging of the white population is a primary reason why racial churning is beginning at younger ages. During the first decade of the 2000s, the number of white youths in the United States already had declined as more individuals aged past eighteen than were born. The white decline is projected to continue not only among children but eventually among younger adults and then middle-aged adults, as smaller white generations follow larger ones.[4] Barring unanticipated increases in white immigration, the long-term scenario for whites is one of lower fertility and greater age. This means that the younger population will lead the way toward the nation's diversity surge. This diversity is already ubiquitous in schools, on playgrounds, and in other civic arenas that young people inhabit. Diversity means that new minorities, including Hispanic and Asian

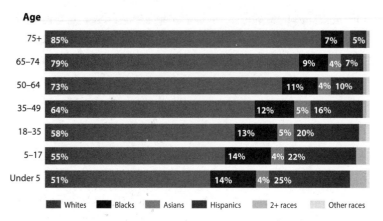

FIGURE 2. Cultural Generation Gap: Population Composition by Age and Race, 2010
Source: Adapted from William H. Frey, *Diversity Explosion: How New Racial Demographics Are Remaking America* (Washington, DC: Brookings Institution Press, 2015).

children whose parents or grandparents came from different nations and speak different languages, will become classmates, dating partners, and lifelong friends with younger generations of established minorities and whites.

Yet this youth-driven diversity surge is also creating a "cultural generation gap" between the diverse youth population and the growing, older, still predominantly white population. (See figure 2.) This gap is reflected in negative attitudes among many older whites toward immigration, new minority growth, and big government programs that cater to the real economic and educational needs of America's younger, more diverse population. It has shown up in politics, among other places, as was evident in the demographic voting patterns in the 2012 election of Barack

Obama. The gap is not a result of racist attitudes per se. It reflects the social distance between minority youth and an older population that does not feel a personal connection with young adults and children who are not "their" children and grandchildren.

Diversity Dispersal "From the Melting Pot Out"

As the diversity surge spreads from younger to older generations, a parallel geographic spread of new minorities is occurring from traditional Melting Pot regions to the rest of the country. This trend is distinct from those of the 1980s and early 1990s, when Hispanic and Asian growth was heavily concentrated in large coastal immigrant gateways such as New York, Los Angeles, San Francisco, Chicago, Miami, and Houston. Those largely immigrant minorities were content to cluster inside the traditional gateways within communities of the same race and language, where they could rely on friendship and family connections for social and economic support. At the same time, most mainstream domestic migrants, primarily whites, were moving to the economically ascendant interior West and Southeast— portions of the country that might be termed the New Sun Belt (shown in figure 3). Being more footloose than the new minorities, these migrants followed growing employment opportunities in places such as Atlanta and Phoenix.

Those separate migration flows—to Melting Pot areas by new immigrant minorities and to New Sun Belt areas by mostly white domestic migrants—seemed to portend a regional demographic balkanization.[5] The scenario painted was one in which the Melting Pot regions would remain racially distinct from other growing parts of the country in much the same way that cities once were racially distinct from their growing suburbs. Such a division

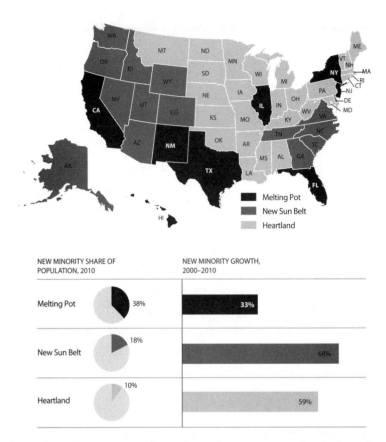

FIGURE 3. New Minorities in the Melting Pot, New Sun Belt, and Heartland Regions
Source: William H. Frey, *Diversity Explosion: How New Racial Demographics Are Remaking America* (Washington, DC: Brookings Institution Press, 2015).

would have extremely adverse implications for racial integration nationally, not to mention for politics.

Fortunately, the predicted balkanization proved temporary. By the late 1990s and early 2000s, new minorities began to follow the broad-based migration flows to the New Sun Belt for many of the same reasons as white domestic migrants. Hispanics and Asians dispersed not only to New Sun Belt states but also to the Heartland region of the country—defined here as slow-growing portions of the nation's interior and New England—in response to jobs in low- and high-skill industries. Like whites and blacks, they wished to escape higher costs of living in many immigrant gateways, and in the process, they began to form new same-race communities away from the Melting Pots.[6]

Yet as they disperse to new destinations, Hispanics, Asians, and other new minorities are not always welcomed with open arms. Although they are filling important niches in the economy by taking jobs in construction, services, and software engineering and are, especially in the Heartland, providing a much-needed increase in population, they also are standing on the front lines of racial integration. White backlash became common in places where the cultural generation gap was most evident and where the growth of young new minorities was most rapid.

Trends toward Integration

The dispersion of new minorities—upward and outward—has also bought signs of greater racial integration—changing long-held stereotypes about who can live where, who can marry whom, and who can be elected to public office.

One such stereotype was the once-common description of urban America as "chocolate cities and vanilla suburbs." Now, white-only flight to the suburbs is a thing of the past. In fact, nearly one-third of large metropolitan suburbs showed a *loss* of whites between 2000 and 2010, and Hispanics are now the biggest drivers of growth of the nation's metropolitan population in both cities and suburbs.[7] Today, it is racial minorities, in their quest for the suburban dream, who are generating new growth and vitality in the suburbs, just as immigrant groups did in the cities in an earlier era. The newest and most notable trend is the accelerated "black flight" to the suburbs. In 2010, for the first time, more blacks lived in the suburbs than in the cities of the biggest U.S. metropolitan regions—joining Hispanics and Asians as well as whites in having that distinction. Although there are vestiges of the old minority city–white suburb residential division, they are largely confined to the slowly growing Heartland. Going forward, suburbs will continue to become a microcosm of a more diverse America, as new generations of suburbanites grow up in communities that bear scant resemblance to suburbia's long-standing white middle-class image.

Residential segregation at the neighborhood level is still high between blacks and whites. Yet, the trends are pointing decidedly away from the highly ghettoized existence that separated blacks from whites for much of the twentieth century. A number of forces—the emergence of a black middle class, black migration to the suburbs and to growing New Sun Belt areas, and integration with new minorities who serve as buffers between racially segregated areas—are leading to continuing and pervasive reductions in black-white segregation.[8] Hispanics and Asians are more likely than blacks to live among whites and other minorities, and both are more likely to reside closer to whites in new destination areas as they disperse across the country. In short, a new racial segregation paradigm appears to be at work that suggests greater residential integration of the races.

Just as long-held stereotypes about where racial groups can live are disappearing, so are those about whom they can marry. Marriages between racial groups were nearly nonexistent as recently as 1970 but the rise of new minorities has changed that dramatically. Today about one in seven new marriages is multiracial, including nearly half of those involving Hispanics or Asians.[9] Even more noteworthy is the increase in marriages between blacks and whites—marriages that would have been illegal in sixteen states as late as 1967. Today black-white marriages are not only accepted but common—composing one-eighth of all marriages involving blacks and almost one-third of *new* marriages involving blacks.

The political impacts of the nation's new diversity surge were made most vivid during the 2008 election of the first black president of the United States and his 2012 reelection. The clout of minorities—both new and old—was responsible for the election and reelection of President Barack Obama.[10] The minority vote was especially crucial for Democrats in 2012, when the Republican candidate, Mitt Romney, lost despite garnering a historically high voting margin among whites. Minority clout can only increase in future elections as more Hispanics and Asians turn age eighteen, register to vote, and turn out to vote. Altogether, these trends foreshadow a continued blurring of racial divisions that would have been unimaginable even a decade ago.

Persisting Economic Divisions

Irrespective of these trends toward greater integration among both new and old minorities, it is important to recognize the continuing sharp social and economic divides that exist between racial minority groups and the generally more advantaged white population.[11] Among Hispanics—especially Mexicans and groups of Central American origin—the gaps with whites are still wide in the areas of education attainment and rate of poverty. Although Asians have been dubbed the "model minority," that is not the case for all Asian groups. Most members of Asian nationalities are first-generation Americans, many of whom need to overcome language and other obstacles in order to translate their training into successful careers. Furthermore, although some strides have been made by new generations of blacks in entering the middle class, a substantial portion of the black population (particularly blacks who are located in isolated residential communities) is still affected by high rates of poverty and unemployment.

The economic disparity due to broader society-wide income and wealth inequality between whites and racial minorities, especially Hispanics and blacks, was exacerbated during the Great Recession of 2007–2009 and its aftermath.[12] For many members of racial minorities, then, there are still major economic barriers that must be overcome if they are to fully assimilate into the American mainstream. Racial discrimination continues to exist, although often in subtler forms than in the past. The landmark 1960s civil rights legislation, enacted during a time of extreme racial discrimination, helped blacks and other minorities improve their economic standing and living conditions to a substantial degree. Given the growing, more diverse racial populations that are central to the nation's future, it is imperative that the kinds of laws and policies put in place to ensure equal access to employment, housing, education, and voting be enforced, monitored, and—where necessary—augmented to accommodate new groups and needs, including the integration of immigrants and their families.

A Demographic Framework for Change

As a demographer, I believe that in periods such as the present, the saying "demography is destiny" is especially relevant. Demography may not fully determine destiny but it will strongly shape the nation's destiny in the decades to come. Because of the ongoing diversity explosion, those communities, organizations, and institutions that hope to improve the well-being and ease the integration of new minorities into mainstream society must understand the key areas in which change will be most effective from a demographic standpoint. To exact maximum change, they need to focus on the younger generations, on new minority destinations, and on ways to narrow the cultural generation gap.

Preparing new generations. The nation's future diversity is best exemplified by the arrival of the first minority-white birth cohort in 2011. Those newborns will continue to age into the country's elementary and secondary schools and eventually into its workforce. The success of these young minorities—with respect to their contributions to the labor force and broader economy as well as their general assimilation into the American mainstream—will affect the nation's future considerably. But to be productive workers and citizens, the next generations will require suitable formal schooling and other training consistent with the nation's long-term needs.

That is true for all members of the coming generations, but particular attention should be paid to young Hispanics. Roughly one-half of today's Hispanic children are second-generation Americans, and a plurality have parents with only a high school education or less.[13] Hispanics continue to make progress in completing high school and in pursuing postsecondary education, a pattern that improves for second-generation Hispanics and for immigrants the longer they stay in the United States.[14] Yet to make progress requires overcoming a number of barriers, including segregated schools and lack of access to affordable postsecondary training.

Despite the ongoing dispersion of Hispanics to new destinations with lower residential segregation levels, a plurality of Hispanic students attend urban school systems that are highly segregated by race and income. A 2012 study by Gary Orfield, a longtime observer of U.S. school segregation trends, concludes that 80 percent of Hispanic students attend majority-nonwhite schools and more than two-fifths attend schools in which whites constitute less than 10 percent of the students. Attendance at schools segregated by race and income reflects other barriers to improved education outcomes, including less-qualified teachers, high levels of teacher turnover, and inadequate facilities and learning materials.[15] Segregated schools are a barrier to Hispanic children, as they have been a continuing barrier for a substantial number of black children who, in past decades, lived in highly ghettoized residential environments. Although black-white residential segregation has begun to decline, many black children remain isolated in segregated schools located in poverty-stricken areas.[16]

Apart from segregated schools at the K–12 level, broader access to training for the future U.S. workforce is an issue. It is projected that the plurality of new jobs—and those that are highest paying—will require postsecondary training. But once again, the trajectory typically followed by Hispanics and blacks contrasts sharply with the one followed by whites. Blacks and Hispanics are far more likely to enroll in two-year colleges and less selective four-year colleges and to have lower rates of completion.[17]

Segregation in low-quality schools and the inaccessibility of postsecondary education and training are just two of the barriers faced by Hispanics, blacks, and other children in today's diverse young student population.[18] Young children and families are central to this discussion, and improvement in access to education is tied to the well-being of minorities and, in fact, of the nation. They are highlighted here because—as in many other areas in which opportunities for future success of minorities can be maximally affected—solutions for improvement are best focused on children and young families.

Preparing new destinations. The spread of Hispanics and Asians to destinations in the New Sun Belt and the Heartland presents opportunities for economic gains in areas that already are growing and in areas that are in need of reinvigoration. The new minority arrivals start out heavily dependent on same-race enclaves for social and economic support and often are viewed with suspicion by long-term residents of a community—a reaction that is self-defeating with respect to the long-term benefit of the community itself.

Spreading out to new areas is especially a challenge for Hispanics, who often are conflated with undocumented immigrants by some long-term residents. Particularly since 2000, many communities have reacted by proposing punitive immigration laws designed to restrict access to housing or employment. Such measures were more pervasive in the New Sun Belt and Heartland regions where the immigrant and Hispanic presence is new and growing.[19]

In these areas in particular, new minority integration into the community is most important. The long-term economic and demographic foundations of these areas can be put in place if existing residents take steps to accommodate new minorities just as these minorities are beginning to establish their presence. This involves providing for their needs with regard to schools, social services, employment assistance, and civic engagement by mounting specialized outreach efforts. A key element in many areas is English language training by public, private, and nonprofit organizations, along with partnerships that match employment opportunities with both high- and low-skilled residents, following the models established in Melting Pot areas.[20]

Bridging the cultural generation gap. Perhaps the biggest demographic fault line in the coming decades will be the cultural generation gap—the lack of intimate connections between an increasingly diverse young population and the mostly white older population. This gap is already evident, demographically, in New Sun Belt states such as Arizona and Nevada where children are a much more racially diverse group than seniors are. But this gap increasingly will spread, along with the dispersal of youthful minorities, to other parts of the New Sun Belt and beyond.

The older generation of whites—today's baby boomers and senior citizens—spent their youth and in some cases early adult years in a nation in which most of the population was white and in which blacks, then the largest minority, resided in heavily segregated neighborhoods. Racially different immigrant groups were few, as most immigrants then were whites from different countries who arrived in the first part of the twentieth century. The older U.S. population has met the growth of new minorities with skepticism.

The young-old gap spills over into politics. The younger population, now heavily composed of minorities, is more likely to favor larger government and support programs such as those that improve education, make housing more affordable, and create jobs. The older boomer population is wary of a bigger federal government (except to preserve the solvency of Social Security) and favors lower taxes. These issues help to explain the sharply divergent voting patterns of seniors and millennials in the 2012 presidential election, in which whites and older adults voted Republican while minorities and young people voted Democratic.[21] These issues will continue to play out at the local level in referendums on expenditures for public schools and for social services for older people.[22]

The emerging political divide between the "gray and the brown," as the political writer Ronald Brownstein describes it, will be counterproductive in the long run.[23] That is because the older, largely white population will need the future minority-dominant adult population to be productive workers, taxpayers, and consumers if the nation's economy is to continue to grow and produce revenues and services that benefit both the young and the old.[24] Both public- and private-sector planning should strive for win-win solutions when interests appear to clash.[25] More important, political, religious, and community leaders in all parts of the country should strive to educate both the young and the old about the need to accommodate each other as part of the emerging demographic transformation.

A Demographic Force That Will Remake America

Despite these economic divides, generational gaps, and the challenges they present, I believe that the demographic die is cast in a way that will ensure that the coming generations of what are now thought of as racial minorities will not just "fit in" but will hold sway in important ways in both public- and private-sector decision making. The economy will wax and wane, as will immigration flows. But through it all, today's minorities—both new and old—will have considerable demographic clout in the nation's politics and economy.

At the time that civil rights legislation was enacted in the 1960s, the mostly black racial minority population accounted for just 15 percent of the total U.S. population and was geographically concentrated in the South and in large cities, mostly in the North and on the West Coast. By 2020, the combined minority groups—including blacks, Hispanics, Asians, American Indians, multiracial individuals, and others—will constitute 40 percent of the U.S. population. These groups already constitute at least two-fifths of the child population in twenty-two states. Therefore future public officials and political candidates at all levels of government, if they are not members of racial minorities themselves, will need to pay close attention to needs and concerns of minority voters, including issues affecting their economic well-being.

It is not just their larger size and increased political clout that will bring greater power to racial minorities. Their potential will be most clearly understood as members of the older white population begin to retire from the labor force, leaving far fewer whites to take their place. Between 2010 and 2030, the primary labor force–age population will experience a net loss of 15 million whites; at the same time, it will gain 26 million racial minorities. All of the latter will be needed, in private- and public-sector jobs in all parts of the country, since the number of workers that the economy is expected to require will far exceed the number needed to replace retiring workers.[26]

Thus, the growth of new minorities from the bottom of the age distribution upward is happening just in time to fill a substantial workforce void. This demographic transformation will also serve to enhance the prospects for minority workers themselves. In *Blurring the Color Line*, the sociologist Richard Alba shows how the opening up of good jobs due to the retirement of baby boomers can provide opportunities for upward mobility for immigrant and second-generation Hispanics and Asians. Moreover, because the new minority workers are replacing and not competing with existing white workers, they will be more readily accepted by their coworkers and by society at large.[27]

There are many other areas in which racial minorities will make their presence felt as they become part of the country's mainstream—as leaders in industry and government, as celebrities in sports and entertainment, and as contributors to the broader popular culture (beyond just youth culture)—as they age further into adulthood. There are several reasons why I foresee their eventual widespread acceptance and assimilation into a new American mainstream.

First, most Americans take pride in the national immigrant heritage, which has been passed down as part of U.S. history, and have learned firsthand the value of immigrants' contributions to the country. Older baby boomers, many descending from European ethnic stock, will—over time—be inclined to accept new minorities from Latin American, Asia, and other national origins as they come to value their contributions to U.S. society. Second, by making racial discrimination unacceptable and the inclusion of racial groups a broadly held social value for most Americans, civil rights legislation itself has had a profound and lasting impact on American sensibilities.[28] Third, the globalization of commerce and communications, expedited by the information technology revolution, will continue to broaden Americans' understanding and acceptance of people from different cultures and nations in ways that would have been impossible to imagine just a decade or two ago.

The foremost reason why I anticipate the integration of both new and old racial minorities into the nation's mainstream is the sheer force of the unprecedented change in the nation's racial demographics. As many more Americans experience day-to-day interactions with members of different racial groups, they will come to value their contributions as coworkers, neighbors, and family members. They will become more willing than ever before to support community, private-sector, and government efforts that foster those groups' interests. The diversity explosion that the country is now experiencing will alter all aspects of society in ways that can help the nation prosper, make it more inclusive, and increase its global connectivity. The 2010 census as well as the 2008 and 2012 presidential elections have made it apparent that the United States is on the cusp of great change—toward a new national demographic transformation in the twenty-first century.

PART ONE
ESSAYS

CHAPTER 1

Less Separate, Still Unequal: Diversity and Equality in "Post–Civil Rights" America

Thomas J. Sugrue

The Paradox of Diversity, Toleration, and Inequality

It is now a commonplace assertion that the United States will be majority nonwhite in a few decades.[1] But that prediction tells us nothing about what diversity will mean, which identities will be salient and which will fade from significance, or how diversity will shape Americans' lives from where they go to school to where and how they live, where they work, what they are paid, if they are healthy or prone to illness, and whether throughout their lives they are treated with dignity and respect. Throughout American history, racial and ethnic categories have profoundly structured educational opportunities, jobs and financial security or insecurity, access to political representation and public goods, and nearly every aspect of the life course, from birth outcomes to health to mortality.

The relationship between race or ethnicity and opportunity is not fixed, however. It has changed at critical junctures during moments of disruption and possibility. When it comes to diversity and equality, the United States now stands at one of those critical junctures, a period when new demographic realities have destabilized old racial categories, when the ideal of diversity and inclusion clashes with xenophobia and exclusion, and when many minorities still suffer constricted opportunities as the result of deeply entrenched historical patterns.

The United States is a more diverse and, at least superficially, a more tolerant society today than it was a half century ago. Overt expressions of racism are less common, even if they have yet to disappear, particularly in the anonymous recesses of the Internet. It is a sign of dramatic change that public figures who express racial biases can expect to be exposed and criticized publicly. Americans have come to expect diversity in the top ranks of government, in newsrooms, and on university faculties, even if those expectations are not always met. College admissions websites regularly feature photos of students of different backgrounds. Both major political parties engage in outreach to nonwhites, with varying degrees of success. Diversity, however, is not a precondition for inclusion or equality. "Increasingly the term *diversity* is paired with the term *inclusion* as if both terms imply each other," the demographer Marta Tienda argues, but "the presumption is unwarranted."[2] Diversity is necessary but far from sufficient to ensure a more just and equal society.

Amidst a shift in professed attitudes and in the public representation of group differences, the United States remains riven by deep patterns of racial, ethnic, and socioeconomic separation and inequality. Residential segregation remains a distinctive feature of the American landscape, even if the forms it takes have changed over the past fifty years. Even if American schools are more diverse than ever (only 54 percent of primary and secondary school students in 2010 were white), public education has resegregated since 1990. Racial and ethnic gaps in education, employment, income and poverty, household wealth, health and access to health care, personal security, and incarceration are deep and persistent. The sociologist Charles Tilly coined the phrase *durable inequalities* to describe the persistence of differences in opportunity across time. Durable inequalities perpetuate social hierarchies. They reinforce advantages for some segments of the population and exacerbate disadvantages for others.[3]

We must account for the paradox that, despite a growing acceptance of the principle of diversity in the United States, American metropolitan areas remain (with regional variation) quite segregated by race and ethnicity and increasingly segregated by income. Those patterns of segregation affect opportunities at every stage of the life course, including access to a high-quality education from primary school through university, job opportunities, household assets, and life expectancies. Segregation has negative feedback loop effects that reinforce inequalities across generations.[4] This paradox raises some troubling questions with normative implications: Is toleration irrelevant to inequality? Does the widely accepted celebration of diversity mask inequality? Do spatialized inequalities—the separation of groups spatially by race and income—impinge on the goal of creating a more unified society?

When the Color of America Changed: Civil Rights and Immigration Reform

To understand the entanglement of growing diversity and entrenched inequality requires a look backward to the last critical juncture in American history when notions of race and citizenship, diversity and tolerance shifted—the civil rights revolution.

Within a few years in the mid-1960s, America's long-standing racial order, one that systematically privileged whites, saw its legislative and legal underpinnings crumble. In July 1964, President Lyndon Johnson signed landmark civil rights legislation, which prohibited discrimination on the basis of race, national origin, sex, religion, and age. That legislation was a first step. In 1965, Johnson signed the Voting Rights Act; in 1968, he and Congress drafted and enacted a law that forbade discrimination in the sale and rental of housing.

Johnson's civil rights laws were not self-enforcing: their success depended on executive orders, federal regulations, and voluntary efforts to break down racial barriers, not to mention the efforts of civil rights groups and often-disruptive protestors to press for change. Nearly every element of the civil rights revolution met with fierce opposition and resistance, as judges, politicians, and policy makers attempted to weaken or roll back civil rights laws, and as ordinary citizens fought against what many called "forced" integration, whether it be efforts to open housing markets, desegregate public schools, or diversify workplaces and colleges. Still, Johnson's law signaled a robust national commitment to the ideals of formal equality and contributed to unprecedented—if often halting—diversification of labor markets, institutions of higher education, and some neighborhoods and schools.

A half century ago, America's color also began to change. In October 1965, at a ceremony at the base of the Statue of Liberty, Johnson signed the Hart-Cellar Act, which lifted immigration restrictions that favored newcomers from northern and western Europe. That year, close to nine in ten Americans were white. The percentage of foreign-born in the United States was at a near low. Unless you lived in California's Central Valley or along the Rio Grande, or found yourself in a handful of neighborhoods like New York's East Harlem, Miami's Little Havana, or East Los Angeles, Hispanics were mostly invisible. The Asian-descended population was vanishingly small, clustered in a few Chinatowns, Little Manilas, and a handful of other enclaves, only a few outside of California.

"The land flourished," stated Johnson, "because it was fed from so many sources—because it was nourished by so many cultures and traditions and peoples."[5] What Johnson had not anticipated was that the nation would be nourished by new cultures and traditions, fewer with European origins. Fifty years after Johnson took office, there were more than 41 million foreign-born people living in the United States, most of them from Latin America, the Caribbean, Africa, and Asia.

Today, whites comprise only 64 percent of the population of the United States. African Americans make up about 13 percent, a slight increase from the civil rights era, in part because of the growth of immigration from the Caribbean and Africa. About half of black Americans live in the South. Most others are concentrated in large metropolitan areas, mainly in the former industrial belt in the Northeast and Midwest.

Nothing has changed the color of America more than the dramatic increase in the Hispanic population.[6] In 1970, 9.6 million Hispanics lived in the United States—about 4 percent of the population. In 2010, that population had increased to 51 million—about 16 percent of the population.[7] It is hard to generalize about Hispanics. The category encompasses people with origins in some twenty countries across three continents and the Caribbean. *Hispanic* (a term that came into official use in the mid-1970s) is not a racial category. Hispanics, by census definition, can be black (like the descendants of enslaved Africans

43

brought to the Dominican Republic, Puerto Rico, or Cuba), white (Spaniards or the descendants of Spanish colonists), American Indian (like Mayans from Mexico or Honduras), or Asian (including Japanese Peruvians or Chinese Cubans). They can also fall into the category "other race." A majority of Hispanics consider themselves white, but in the 2010 census, more Hispanics than ever checked the box "other race," signaling their dissatisfaction with existing racial categories.

Sixty-five percent of Hispanics in the United States today are of Mexican descent and another 9 percent hail from Puerto Rico. The next largest groups—Cubans, Salvadorans, Dominicans, and Guatemalans—together make up another 14 percent. Their reasons for coming to the United States are as diverse as their national origins. Some Mexicans came to the United States as migratory farmworkers and, on a smaller scale, industrial workers in the twentieth century, though many were temporary sojourners in the United States, often part of a circular migration between Mexico and the United States. A small number of Hispanics within the boundaries of the United States descend from families that date back to the Spanish empire (sometimes called Tejanos, Hispanos, and Californios). Cubans almost all came as refugees, some airlifted to the United States, others (more recently) fleeing their homeland by boat or raft. Overall, Hispanic migrants and immigrants tend to be quite heterogeneous in terms of their national origins, their places of arrival, their educational capital, and their place in the racial hierarchy of the United States.[8]

Hispanics live in every state, with some of the fastest growth happening in places remote from the traditional immigrant gateways of California, Texas, and Florida. Guatemalans work in the chicken processing plants of North Carolina; Mexicans in the meatpacking factories of Iowa and Kansas; Hondurans and Mexicans as landscapers and construction workers in central New Jersey. Hardly any neighborhood on Chicago's North and West Sides does not have an immigrant-run taqueria or a corner bodega.

The aggregate statistics do not reflect significant regional variation. The western states (particularly California) are far more diverse than other parts of the United States. Forty-seven percent of residents of that region are nonwhite. The population of the Midwest is the least diverse, but still 22 percent of its population is nonwhite. Between the two are the Northeast (31 percent nonwhite) and the South (40 percent nonwhite). Metropolitan areas with populations of a half million or more are also far more diverse than smaller cities and towns.[9]

Johnson and his contemporaries could not have imagined America's new polychromatic landscape. Latino, white, and Asian teenagers intermingle in shopping malls in Orange County, California, a place that had been a haven for hundreds of thousands of whites fleeing Los Angeles during the 1950s and 1960s. The sight of black-and-white couples holding hands is no longer scandalous in Atlanta. When a firm in Detroit hires new black workers, whites do not engage in wildcat strikes as they did during and after World War II. Real estate brokers in Seattle can show houses to Chinese American homebuyers without fear of alienating their white customers.

One of the most unexpected changes over the past half century has been the rise of suburban diversity. More than half of all Latin American immigrants reside in suburbs. The diverse Asian population—dominated by immigrants from China, India, and Vietnam—comprises 5 percent of U.S. residents. They too have scattered far and wide, most living in the suburbs. African

American suburbanization has also increased steadily during this period, with 51 percent living in the suburbs today. No one in 1964 could have predicted that postwar suburbs, which had been built on the foundation of white racial exclusivity, would become polychromatic and multilingual.[10]

The America that dawned in the 1960s is far more diverse, but it is far from inclusive or equal. Lifting the formal barriers of discrimination did not necessarily make institutions more inclusive, neighborhoods and schools more integrated, or workplaces more representative of the nation's diverse population. The subsequent half century was one of gains and setbacks, of expanding opportunities and still-wrenching injustices, of disadvantages by race and ethnicity sometimes overcome, but just as often intensified and compounded. If the arc of history bent toward justice, it just as often veered off course. To complete the unfinished business of the 1960s means coming to grips with what has changed and what has not, to be attentive to the paradoxes of diversity and inequality, of inclusion and exclusion, of integration and fragmentation.

Where We Live: Still Separate and Unequal

Americans may value diversity as a principle, but in practice they continue to live separate lives. Rates of residential segregation by race and ethnicity have remained stubbornly high in most American metropolitan areas, particularly in areas with large populations of African Americans. Sixty years after the landmark *Brown v. Board of Education* decision, public schools are resegregating by black and white. Latinos face less residential segregation than African Americans, but are now more likely to be concentrated in separate schools, unequal and impoverished.

By nearly every measure, educational and residential segregation ensures that racial inequality in the United States has remained durable.

The segregation of populations by race and income reinforces inequalities through the uneven distribution of public goods, economic resources, hazards, and political power across space. In the United States, where you live determines your access to jobs, your transit options, the quality of public services and how much you pay for them in the form of taxes, your health, and your personal security. Residential segregation by race has contributed to the most durable of inequalities in modern America: the huge racial gaps in household wealth. The result is durable inequalities in academic achievement. Segregation and separation can sometimes be a communal resource, solidifying group bonds and fostering a sense of commonality, but they also exacerbate intergroup conflict, misinformation, and distrust.

Black and White: Enduring Residential Segregation

Blacks and whites in the United States still live largely separate lives. Between the 1920s and the 1990s, the residential segregation of blacks and whites worsened in nearly every American metropolitan area, despite the passage of federal, state, and local laws that forbade discrimination in the sale or rental of housing, and even though public opinion surveys since the 1960s have shown significant, positive shifts in every measure of racial "toleration," including the willingness to live in racially mixed neighborhoods, to support racially diverse schools, and to accept interracial marriage. Since the 1960s, it has become commonplace for Americans to express support for the ideal of "colorblindness," but when it comes to housing and neighborhoods, color still matters greatly.

Segregation did not have a single cause. In the postwar years, it resulted from a combination of public policy and private practices. Federal homeownership programs—the Home Owners Loan Corporation, the Federal Housing Administration, and the Veterans Administration—made insured mortgages available at a low cost to whites, but discouraged lending in neighborhoods that had even a small number of nonwhites. Real estate brokers openly discriminated against people of color. After 1968, civil rights legislation forbade discrimination in home sales, rentals, and lending, but dozens of studies showed that minorities and whites had very different experiences with the real estate market.

African American homebuyers were likely to be steered to neighborhoods of older housing stock, often in declining central cities or fading suburbs, places where housing values often stagnated or depreciated. Since the 1970s, audit studies (with matched pairs of white and minority testers) have shown that steering has remained a persistent issue. Explicit discrimination—being turned away by brokers or landlords—is less common, but a recent Department of Housing and Urban Development study shows that about one in four African Americans report that they have faced discrimination in the rental or purchase of a home.[11] African Americans inquiring about homes or apartments are sometimes rebuffed because of their accents.[12]

African Americans, if they were lucky enough to be homeowners, remained confined to neighborhoods on the margins, economically and politically. One of the legacies of discriminatory real estate and home finance policies was that both whites and minorities came to see the racial separation of metropolitan areas as natural, as the sum of individual choices rather than the deliberate result of prosegregative policies and practices. Racial segregation seemed simply to be the natural order of things: "birds of a feather flock together."

Still, between 1990 and 2010, black-white residential segregation declined modestly in most metropolitan areas. This is a hopeful sign, but it is far too soon to predict whether the trend will continue. The most commonly used metric of segregation—the index of dissimilarity—shows that about six in ten black Americans would have to move for the black and white population to be dispersed evenly across American metropolitan areas. The least segregated areas are those with small black populations, particularly in the Mountain West. Those places are less likely to be scarred by a long history of black-white hostility. And there, the black population is too small for whites to perceive it as threatening. By contrast, black-white segregation has fallen most slowly in the metropolitan areas with the largest black populations—particularly in the Northeast and Midwest. The sociologist Douglas Massey writes that, of African Americans living in metropolitan areas, nearly half live in conditions of hypersegregation, in homogeneous neighborhoods where contact with members of other groups is uncommon.[13]

Of all racial groups, whites are most likely to live in racially homogeneous communities and least likely to come into contact with people unlike themselves. In 2010, the average white lived in a neighborhood that was three-quarters white. One widely used index of segregation measures isolation—that is, the unlikelihood of intergroup contact within neighborhoods. By this measure, whites are the most isolated of racial groups. As a result, write Massey and Rugh, "the vast majority of whites do not experience the rising racial-ethnic diversity of contemporary America."[14]

It is telling that cities that are home to military bases and universities are the most integrated, in large part because they are home to the only two truly diverse American institutions. Their histories are instructive. In the aftermath of President Truman's 1948 executive order desegregating the armed services, the military became the most racially heterogeneous institution in the United States. By the 1960s, the Army, and to a lesser extent the Navy and Air Force, put a priority on diversifying the ranks of its officers. By the 1980s, the military academies and officer training schools aggressively groomed minorities for leadership positions. The relatively equal interaction of blacks and whites in the military and around military bases also led to higher rates of interracial marriage.[15] Universities in most of the country also made efforts, beginning in the 1960s, to diversity their student bodies. Some—mostly in the South—were compelled to do so to remedy past discrimination in the aftermath of the 1960s civil rights legislation and civil rights litigation. Other institutions developed voluntary programs to consider race and ethnicity as plus factors in admissions. Prodiversity initiatives changed the color of many universities and their surrounding communities, but those gains were fragile, and did not necessarily accomplish the goal of full incorporation and inclusion.[16]

Hispanics: Rising and Falling Segregation

In the most comprehensive overview of Hispanic residential patterns, Mary Fischer and Marta Tienda describe the "paradox of rising and falling segregation across metropolitan areas."[17] In the aggregate, whites and Hispanics are less likely to live apart than whites and African Americans, reflecting the ways that native-born Americans have long seen Hispanics as an "in-between group." Residential segregation is lower for those who arrive in parts of the country with relatively few Hispanics, and for those who arrive in cities with only small African American populations. Rates of segregation are generally lower for second- and third-generation Hispanics, and in those metropolitan areas that have longer-established Hispanic populations.

There are, however, two noteworthy exceptions to the pattern of lower rates of segregation among Hispanics, and they are revealing. Afro-Hispanics, mostly Puerto Rican, Dominican, and Colombian, tend to live in highly segregated neighborhoods, often in close proximity to African Americans.[18] New Hispanic immigrants are also likely to live in highly segregated communities. Segregation rates are highest in gateway cities with large Hispanic populations. Nearly 20 percent of Hispanics living in metropolitan areas live in hypersegregated neighborhoods, most of them in New York City (where much of the Hispanic population is of African descent) and in Los Angeles (the metropolitan area with both the largest number of Hispanics and the greatest number of new arrivals).[19]

In some cities, Hispanics serve as "buffers" between black and white neighborhoods, diversifying both. But there is also substantial evidence that Hispanics are reluctant to move to predominantly African American neighborhoods. In their study of ethnic neighborhoods in Los Angeles, Lawrence Bobo and Camille Charles found that newly arriving immigrants from Latin America quickly define themselves as "not black." They are attracted to neighborhoods with substantial white populations and view the presence of even a modest number of African Americans as a sign that a neighborhood is troubled or in decline.[20] William Julius Wilson and Richard Taub have found similar patterns in Chicago.[21]

It is difficult to predict the future direction of Hispanic residential segregation. If Latin American, Caribbean, and South American immigration slows, it is likely that segregation rates will drop. And if current patterns hold, Hispanic-white residential segregation should continue to decline as the native-born Hispanic population grows.[22] Rising intermarriage rates between Hispanics and whites may also result in a blurring of ethnoracial distinctions and a decline in residential segregation.[23] But the growing hypersegregation in New York and Los Angeles serves as a cautionary tale: residential integration is not inevitable.[24]

Unequal Education

In 1965, less than a year after he signed the Civil Rights Act, and just months before he signed the voting rights and immigration reform legislation, Lyndon Johnson signed the Elementary and Secondary Education Act of 1965. That landmark legislation substantially stepped up federal investment in public education, but with three overriding purposes. First was to bolster the role of schools in providing students with the intellectual tools to adapt to a rapidly evolving labor market that put a premium on high degrees of literacy, numeracy, and technical knowledge. Second was to level the playing field between rich and poor students. The third was to break down the long-standing barriers of race that had confined African Americans, and to a lesser degree Hispanics, to second-class schools.

A half century later, public schools remain divided by race, ethnicity, and socioeconomic status. Many children leave school ill-prepared for higher education and without the skill sets necessary for success in an increasingly high-tech economy. Education research has shown consistently that majority-minority schools face one of several problems. They are almost always underfunded in comparison to schools in nearby majority-white districts. They face high teacher turnover and have a harder time attracting credentialed teachers. They are more likely to have superannuated facilities and outdated classroom materials. Most significantly, their students tend to be disproportionately poor, lacking the familial resources and the cultural capital to do well in the classroom.

The Resegregation of African American Education

While rates of black-white residential segregation have fallen modestly since 1990, over the same period, American public schools have resegregated. The process of resegregation has unraveled many of the gains of the civil rights era. By the 1950s, most northern states had outlawed separate "Negro" or "colored" schools, but new patterns of segregation that were even more effective took their place. Within districts, school attendance zones usually corresponded closely to a neighborhood's racial composition. As "neighborhood schools" came under legal challenge in dozens of court cases and voluntary desegregation plans in the 1960s, 1970s, and 1980s, many white parents voted with their feet and moved across school district boundaries, leading to an increase in interdistrict segregation at the same time that intradistrict segregation was declining.

Until 1954, racially separate schools were required by law throughout the former Confederacy (in South Texas, schools separated whites from both African Americans and Mexican Americans). In the wake of civil rights legislation in the 1960s, many southern school districts introduced neighborhood schools as part of a strategy to resist school desegregation by making the case that school attendance zones were race neutral in design.

Efforts to break down segregation *within* school districts throughout the country were most successful in the period between 1970 and 1990. In many northern states, departments of education required districts to implement "racial balance" plans to break down long-standing patterns of racial segregation. Some districts also implemented their own voluntary desegregation plans, in part to avoid civil rights lawsuits. Many districts, particularly in the South, were under court order to desegregate. Whether by administrative fiat or court order, districts slowly integrated by shifting school attendance zones, creating citywide magnet schools, or consolidating racially segregated schools. As a result, school districts across the country grew less segregated.[25]

School districts that spanned whole counties, nearly all of them in the Sun Belt, most successfully integrated.[26] By the 1980s, Southern public schools that spanned whole counties (including Nashville, Jacksonville, and Raleigh) were among the most racially diverse in the country. In these school districts, educational segregation fell sharply, in large part because whites lacked the opportunity to jump across municipal boundaries to towns with better-funded white-majority schools. In Charlotte, North Carolina, to take a prominent example, the school district spanned a central city, historically segregated black and white urban neighborhoods, public housing projects, postwar suburbs, and even semirural areas. After the Supreme Court's 1972 *Swann v. Charlotte-Mecklenburg* ruling, Charlotte's schools desegregated rapidly and racial gaps in achievement narrowed considerably.[27]

Interdistrict segregation—particularly in the fragmented metropolitan areas in the Northeast and Midwest—proved to be far more resistant to change. Black-white segregation between districts had risen steadily during the postwar period, largely because of white flight from racially mixed central cities to homogeneous suburban school districts. The U.S. Supreme

Court also put up a nearly insuperable hurdle to interdistrict desegregation in its 1974 *Milliken v. Bradley* decision, which struck down a fifty-three-district desegregation plan in metropolitan Detroit on the grounds that suburban school districts had not engaged in intentional racial segregation and hence could not be responsible for remedying it.[28]

The gains of the post–civil rights years proved to be very fragile. Beginning in the 1990s, American schools began to resegregate by race and grow more stratified by class.[29] That process accelerated—particularly in the South—at the turn of the century, as parents (many migrants from the hypersegregated North) began to lobby for homogeneous neighborhood schools and because federal courts began to roll back metropolitan-wide school desegregation plans.[30] The Charlotte experiment in desegregation, for example, ended after a 1999 federal court ruling that the district was "unitary" and no longer needed to implement its desegregation plan. Charlotte quickly resegregated. More recently, in the 2007 *Parents Involved* case, the conservative majority on the Supreme Court struck down as unconstitutional voluntary school desegregation programs in Louisville, Kentucky, and Seattle, Washington, and threatened similar programs elsewhere.[31] A small number of districts, like Wake County (Raleigh), North Carolina, have attempted to replace race-sensitive enrollment policies with programs to foster socioeconomic integration. But such efforts to break down class-stratified school districts have also met with fierce resistance from better-off parents, most of them white.[32]

The consequence is that nearly three-quarters of African American students today attend majority-nonwhite schools, and 38 percent attend schools with student bodies that are 10 percent or less white.[33] Black students are also far more likely than whites to attend schools where many of their classmates live in poverty. Black students attended schools where 64 percent of their classmates were eligible for reduced-price or free lunch programs (a proxy for poverty). The combination of racial isolation and concentrated poverty has negative impacts on educational outcomes.[34]

Within public schools, particularly those that are highly segregated by race, black students (especially young men) have been subject to new, punitive forms of discipline. Even though juvenile crime rates have fallen steadily since the mid-1990s, school disciplinary procedures have grown increasingly harsh. The use of suspensions to punish students has skyrocketed in the past forty years, disproportionately affecting black students. In 2011–2012, black students made up 16 percent of those enrolled in schools nationwide, but 32 percent of those who received in-school suspensions, 33 percent of those who received out-of-school suspensions, 42 percent of those suspended more than once, and 34 percent of those expelled. Black students are also disproportionately subject to "zero tolerance" policies that require schools to report even minor fights and other disciplinary infractions to law enforcement officials; 27 percent of students referred to law enforcement officials are blacks, twice their representation in the population of enrolled students. Suspensions and zero tolerance have had perverse effects on educational outcomes: students who are suspended or expelled are less likely to graduate and more likely to be incarcerated later. Disciplinary policies also contribute to a growing gender imbalance in high school completion rates among black students, leading to a sizable gender gap in college enrollments and growing disparities in labor force participation between black men and women.

Overall, African Americans are still less likely than whites to attend institutions of higher education and, even when they do attend college, less likely to graduate. In 2010, only a little more than 19 percent of blacks had college degrees.[35]

Hispanic Education: Growing Segregation

More than a quarter of all K–12 students in the United States today are Hispanic, with the greatest percentages in the states that border Mexico; 60 percent of students enrolled in New Mexico's schools are Hispanic; in California, more than 50 percent; in Texas, almost 49 percent; and in Arizona, 41 percent. Across the country, Hispanic students face more segregation than ever; indeed, Hispanic students are more likely today than even African Americans to attend racially segregated schools. As William Frey points out in this volume, 80 percent of Hispanic students attend schools where half or more of their classmates are nonwhite; 43 percent attend schools where less than 10 percent of their fellow students are white. In addition, schools that serve Hispanic students tend to be disproportionately poor: the average Hispanic student attends a school in which nearly two-thirds of students are in poverty.[36]

Court-ordered and voluntary school desegregation programs seldom affected Hispanics. The *Keyes* case (a 1973 Supreme Court ruling that ordered the desegregation of the Denver public schools) was one of the few educational civil rights cases to consider Hispanics at all, and it had little influence beyond that district.[37] The dramatic growth of the Hispanic school-age population after 1990 coincided with federal courts' rollback of court-ordered and voluntary desegregation efforts. Because Hispanic children are more likely than blacks or whites to attend schools in countywide districts, they experience more intradistrict segregation (confined to neighborhood schools) than interdistrict segregation.[38]

Many school districts, particularly in suburbs and smaller towns, have struggled to adapt to shifting demographics and the distinctive educational needs of nonnative students. Eighty-three percent of foreign-born Hispanic children speak Spanish solely or primarily at home, and 54 percent of native-born Hispanic children with immigrant parents speak Spanish at home.[39] But many teachers (especially in schools that transitioned quickly from white to Hispanic) lack the training to meet their students' linguistic needs. In parts of the country that are part of the far-flung "New Latino diaspora," receiving new immigrants for the first time, many school districts have inadequate resources or lack the political will to develop bilingual education programs, to incorporate immigrant parents into decisions involving their students, to train teachers about the culture of newcomers, and to refine curricula to meet the needs of a multicultural student body. Anti-immigrant sentiment on school boards, among teachers, and among native-born parents can compound Hispanic students' educational disadvantages.[40]

Educational data show positive changes in recent years, particularly in school attendance and completion rates. Students of all backgrounds are much more likely to graduate from high school than ever before. The decline in dropouts has been particularly pronounced for Hispanic students. Between 1972 (the first year that data were compiled) through 2002, between 25 and 35 percent of Hispanic students ages 16–24 dropped out of high school. That figure plummeted between 2003 and 2013, when 13 percent of Hispanic students ages 16–24 dropped out.

Still, that figure is high compared to the 4 percent of whites and 8 percent of blacks who leave high school without a diploma.[41]

The disadvantages of attending segregated, poorly resourced public schools, often with teachers ill-trained to respond to immigrant children, leaves Hispanics at a disadvantage in postsecondary education: on average their test scores and grade point averages are lower. Hispanics are underrepresented among those attending college (in part because of barriers to admission and financial aid, especially for undocumented immigrants). Hispanic students are more likely than other groups to attend nonselective colleges. From the community colleges to research universities, many institutions of higher education lack support services for Hispanic students. They are more likely to drop out of college, for a mix of personal reasons (including working to pay for tuition or provide financial support to their families) and academic reasons (failing to thrive in college-level classes). Overall, Hispanics are less likely to earn college degrees than other ethnic groups. In 2010, only 13.2 percent of Hispanics had graduated from college. Over time, the lack of college degrees could be a severe impediment to Hispanics' economic advancement. The economic returns to higher education have increased substantially in the past half century and most of the best-paying jobs are closed to those without college degrees.[42]

Making Ends Meet: Persistent Income Inequality

For most of American history, minorities have remained concentrated in the poorest-paying, least secure, and most dangerous or unpleasant jobs. They have also been most vulnerable to unemployment and underemployment. The gap in educational attainment is a particularly important factor in explaining these patterns: those with less education are most likely to be concentrated at the bottom of the occupational ladder. As a consequence, African American and Hispanic incomes remain lower than those of whites. And since the 1970s, there has been very little change in the black-white and black-Hispanic income ratios. Minorities are also particularly vulnerable to falling into poverty. Low income, persistent gaps in the minority-white income ratios, and higher rates of poverty all contribute to greater disadvantages for African Americans and Hispanics at all stages of the life course, but particularly for minority children who are especially likely to spend their formative years in poverty and, over time, to bear the costs of impoverishment. Narrowing the income gap is essential for the full incorporation and inclusion of nonwhite groups in American society.

The Ongoing Black Employment Crisis

Blacks were far more likely than whites to be unemployed. Black unemployment rates have remained one-and-a-half to two times that of whites since the 1950s—regardless of the state of the economy, in part because of their residential concentration in places that have been most ravaged by macroeconomic changes.[43] Rural southern blacks are concentrated in places that have weak economies, where agricultural jobs disappeared long ago. Many industrial employers that moved southward concentrated facilities in places with substantial white populations but relatively few African Americans (such as the South Carolina Piedmont or central Tennessee). The northern cities that attracted the largest African American populations were those most ravaged by deindustrialization. The suburbanization of employment—but not of minority housing and transportation—further hindered job opportunities for blacks. The notion of the "spatial mismatch," first developed in the 1960s to describe the gap between prospective workers and jobs, still has salience, particularly in sprawling metropolitan areas where job growth has been most robust on the periphery but housing choices remain constrained and public transit systems weak or underfunded. The only bright light in many places—particularly in the urban north—was the expansion of public-sector employment in the post-1960s period. By the best available estimate, 40 percent of the African American middle class worked for government or for firms that relied on government contracts.

African American men have the lowest rates of labor force participation of any group. There is no single explanation for the enormous racial disparities in employment prospects. Despite decades of antidiscrimination legislation, race and ethnicity still matter greatly in the hiring process. Interviews and surveys with employers conducted over the past twenty years consistently show that employers consider race, gender, ethnicity, and place of residence when making hiring decisions.[44] For many employers race is a "signal" of a potential employee's personal character. Drawing from racial stereotypes, employers make assumptions about individuals' work ethic, promptness, self-discipline, and productivity. In one study, economists found that job applicants with names like Emily and Greg were more likely to be hired than those with comparable credentials named Lakisha and Jamal.[45]

Huge racial disparities in incarceration also play a key role in constricting job opportunities, especially for African American men. Since 1970, the number of Americans imprisoned has quadrupled. Today, six in ten prisoners are African American or Hispanic. A major reason for the growth in the carceral state was the war on drugs. In 1970, about 322,300 Americans were arrested on drug-related charges, compared to more than 1,375,600 in 2000.[46] That war was fought most intensely in minority communities. Black males are incarcerated at 6.5 times the rate of white males. Hispanic males are 2.6 times more likely than whites to be incarcerated.[47] Many employers are unwilling to hire men with a criminal record, and some jobs, particularly involving personal care, are closed to felons. It is now commonplace for firms to conduct criminal background checks on job applicants. The sociologist Devah Pager found that ex-offenders were 60 percent less likely than those without a criminal record to be called back after a job interview. The mark of race doubly stigmatizes black ex-offenders: they are far less likely than their white counterparts to be considered for a job.[48]

Hispanics: Employed, but in Dead-End Jobs

By contrast, Hispanic labor force participation rates are high. The same employers who are often skeptical of hiring African Americans are often attracted to Latin American immigrants, imputing to them the qualities of hard work and the willingness to work long hours. Latinos tend to be concentrated in unskilled jobs, especially in construction, maintenance and household work, low-level health and personal care jobs, and repair work. In old industrial cities, like Chicago and Philadelphia, where the number of manufacturing jobs has steadily declined, the proportion of Hispanic workers holding those jobs has increased. Employers in low-wage industries, especially food processing, also rely extensively on undocumented workers to keep wages low. Those employers frequently disregard laws that require immigrants to provide proof of their work eligibility, taking advantage of the fact that undocumented workers are unlikely to jeopardize their employment and immigration status by demanding better wages and working conditions.

The concentration of Hispanics in bottom-tier jobs has three significant effects. First, few of these jobs offer ladders for advancement. They offer few opportunities for income growth, skill enhancement, and upward mobility. Second, many Hispanic households must rely on the income of more than one family member to make ends meet, a decision that sometimes encourages college-aged children to forgo further education because their families depend on their income. Third, those jobs do not usually offer long-term benefits and insurance, meaning that disabled and elderly workers are particularly vulnerable economically.

Income Gaps and Poverty

Both African Americans and Hispanics earn significantly less than whites. The income gap between black and white households narrowed during the decade following the passage of civil rights legislation. Black households earned 55 percent of white households in 1967; in 2013, they earned 59 percent of white households. The .59 income ratio between blacks and whites has remained constant since 1973. The gap in household income reflects, in large part, the large number of single-earner African American households.[49]

For all of the media attention lavished on black celebrities and on black urban professionals and suburbanizing middle-class blacks, even the best-off African Americans are not as rich as whites. As Patrick Sharkey has shown, the share of blacks in the top quintile of American income earners has barely changed over the past forty years, from 8 percent in 1970 to 9 percent in 2011. By contrast, blacks have remained overrepresented among the poorest Americans. At the beginning of the 1970s, 39 percent of African Americans were in the poorest quintile of income earners; forty years later, 33 percent were. Over the same period, the percentage of African Americans in the poorest two quintiles only fell from 65 to 58 percent.[50]

The civil rights era witnessed dramatic drops in poverty, in particular for African Americans. The rate of black poverty fell by half between 1959 and 2013, with the sharpest declines in the 1960s, a combination of the strong national economy, the gains attendant on civil rights legislation, and the expansion of eligibility for federal income support programs. In 1959, 55 percent of blacks lived below the poverty line. Ten years later, only 33 percent were poor. Between 1970 and 1994, black poverty rates hovered around one-third. They dropped below 30 percent for the first time in 1995, falling to a record low of 22 percent in 2001. Black poverty rates slowly crept back upward, and exceeded 27 percent in 2013.[51]

The socioeconomic status of Hispanics is, in some respects, better than that of African Americans. Hispanic household income is higher than that of blacks (it reached $40,963 in 2013, compared to $34,598 for African Americans, $58,270 for non-Hispanic whites, and $67,065 for Asians). The difference between black and Hispanic household income reflects in part the fact that many Hispanic households rely on the wages of more than one worker, whereas African American households are more likely to have a single income earner. Still, the white-Hispanic income gap has remained persistently large. The ratio of Hispanic to white household income was .74 in 1972. It fell by 2013 to .70.[52]

Hispanic household income varies by place of origin. Using data from the late 1990s and early 2000s, Cordelia Reimers found that Dominicans had the lowest annual household income, followed by Mexicans, other Central Americans, and Puerto Ricans. But second- and third-generation Hispanics of all groups saw their household incomes and per capita incomes increase significantly. Non-Hispanic whites earned more at the household and individual levels than did Hispanics of any origin, but by the second generation, both the household and per capita income of all Hispanics surpassed that of African Americans and moved closer to that of whites.[53]

Poverty also remains a problem for Hispanics across the life course. In 2013, 23.5 percent of Hispanics lived below the poverty line. While they constituted 16 percent of the U.S. population in 2013, more than 28 percent of the poor in the United States were Hispanic. Poverty among Hispanics is particularly high among two groups: children (about 30 percent of whom live beneath the poverty line) and the elderly (about 20 percent of those over 65 are poor), in large part because citizenship or work status excluded them from Social Security or Medicare, which have played a crucial role in lifting many older Americans out of poverty.[54]

Growing Wealth Gaps

No racial gap is more pronounced than that in household wealth. The black-white wealth gap offers the clearest example of the impact of history on the present, what sociologists Melvin Oliver and Thomas Shapiro call the "sedimentation of racial inequality." They conclude that "blacks' socioeconomic status results from a socially layered accumulation of disadvantages passed on from generation to generation."[55]

A household's wealth might include bank accounts, stocks, securities, and bonds, retirement plans, ownership of a small business, and items of rapidly depreciating value like cars. For most households, real estate is the largest asset. Homeowners can use the equity in their real estate to get access to home improvement loans, to refinance at beneficial terms, to pay for college tuition, and to pass on inheritances to their children. Historical wealth gaps, in particular, have cumulative impacts. As Oliver and Shapiro write, "whites in general, but well-off whites in particular, were able to amass assets and use their secure financial status to pass their wealth from generation to generation."

Blacks and Hispanics are less likely to own their own homes than whites (currently 43 percent of blacks, 46 percent of Hispanics, and 73 percent of whites are homeowners).[56] Those minorities who do own homes are more likely to have less equity in their properties, pay higher interest rates, and own properties in communities where property values have remained low.

The gaps in homeownership and real estate values are both the long-term results of discriminatory real estate practices dating back to the New Deal; the long-term process of institutional and commercial disinvestment in minority neighborhoods; formal and informal restrictions that closed minorities out of conventional and federal government–backed mortgage markets; discrimination by real estate brokers; and, most recently, predatory lending practices.

Around the turn of the twenty-first century, there sprang up a huge new industry of predatory lenders that targeted members of minority groups, including those who already owned their homes and who were persuaded to refinance on what turned out to be usurious terms. In 2006, more than half of subprime loans went to African Americans, who comprised only 13 percent of the population. And a recent study of data from the Home Mortgage Disclosure Act found that 32.1 percent of blacks, but only

10.5 percent of whites, got higher-priced mortgages—those with an interest rate three or more points higher than the rate of a Treasury security of the same length.

Economist Carolina Reid estimates that nearly 25 percent of African Americans and Latinos who bought or refinanced their homes during the last years of the housing bubble, between 2004 and 2008, have already or will end up losing their homes to foreclosure. Gaps between white and minority borrowers persisted even among the wealthiest borrowers. Only 4.6 percent of higher-income white borrowers lost their homes to foreclosures, compared to 10 percent of higher-income African Americans and 15 percent of higher-income Hispanics.[57]

Data about race, ethnicity, and wealth tell a disheartening story. Between 1984 and 2009, racial gaps between whites and both African Americans and Latinos remained large, but the gaps narrowed, particularly during the mid-1990s. In 1984, whites held a 12–1 wealth advantage over blacks, and an 8–1 advantage over Hispanics. In 1995, the wealth gap between whites and both blacks and Hispanics narrowed to a low of 7–1. The gap, however, widened again, in part because of racial disparities in indebtedness exacerbated by the loosening of credit and the expansion of predatory lending practices beginning in the late 1990s.[58]

The economic crisis beginning in 2007 had a particularly pronounced effect on Latinos and African Americans. A report by the Pew Charitable Trusts found that Hispanic households saw a 66 percent decline in median household wealth between 2005 and 2009; blacks saw a 53 percent decline; and whites a 16 percent decline. The typical black household had only $5,677 in wealth; Hispanics had $6,325. Whites, by contrast, had household wealth of $113,149. In other words, the typical white household was twenty times wealthier than the typical black or Hispanic household.[59]

Assets matter at every stage of the life cycle. They can serve as collateral for car and home loans. They provide parents with resources to help pay for their children's college educations. They can be tapped as seed money to launch a small business, or to pay for costly health care, or retirement expenses. And they can, of course, be passed down to the next generation in the form of inheritances (36 percent of whites but only 7 percent of blacks receive any inheritance, with whites receiving ten times the amount of inheritance).[60] The result is the intergenerational transmission of advantage in the case of whites, and disadvantage among minorities.

The Future of Diversity and Inequality

Will America really be a majority minority country in twenty-five or thirty years? The answer ultimately depends on whether or not the category "majority" remains stable. It depends on the extent to which groups currently categorized as nonwhite are incorporated into the nation's economy and polity. It depends on whether or not current patterns of racialized inequality harden or soften. It depends on whether residential segregation declines, remains stable, or increases. It depends on whether American schools encourage diversity and reflect it in their enrollments, or whether education in the United States remains separate and unequal. It depends on whether sharp racial disparities in income, wealth, employment, and education remain in place, or whether those gaps narrow.

Scholars of race, ethnicity, and immigration suggest several possibilities. Some racial optimists argue that the United States is moving toward a "postethnic" regime, where assimilation rather than racialization is the norm. Some optimists point to the small but steady growth in black-white intermarriage rates since the 1960s as a portent of the blurring of the black-white divide. High rates of intermarriage between second- and third-generation Hispanics and whites may lead to a decline in the power of Hispanicity as a category. Perhaps Hispanics will become white, in a process of assimilation analogous to that of Italians or other southern and eastern European immigrants, once perceived as less than white, in the 1890–1950 period.[61]

Other scholars suggest that persistent educational and residential segregation, as well as wealth and income gaps between blacks, Hispanics, and whites will perpetuate racial and ethnic division and fragmentation, hardening group differences over time. Perhaps the United States is witnessing the rise of a "new Jim Crow," evidenced by the overrepresentation of African Americans among the poor, educationally disadvantaged, and incarcerated.[62] Pessimists also point to the deep anti-immigrant sentiment in American politics, the growth in Hispanic hyper-segregation, and the increase in the number of Hispanics attending segregated schools to predict that Hispanics will not soon, if ever, be incorporated into the American majority. As Tienda and Fuentes suggest, "Hispanics' metropolitan profile has evolved in profound ways that call into question initial optimism that spatial assimilation is ineluctable."[63]

Others suggest, extrapolating from the growing number of Hispanics who select "other race" on the U.S. Census, that Hispanics will emerge as a third racial category in the United States, remaining perpetually in between African Americans and whites. Eduardo Bonilla-Silva suggests that a Latinized scheme of racialization—with a more elaborate system of color gradation than has prevailed in most of the United States—will supplant the "one drop rule" of racial classification, with darker-skinned racial minorities remaining stigmatized and overrepresented among the socioeconomically disadvantaged.[64]

The color of America will certainly continue to change, but the meaning of race and ethnicity in the future will depend to a great extent on policy decisions made today. The inequitable distribution of resources across metropolitan space and by race and ethnicity has created durable inequalities. To challenge those inequalities requires greater attentiveness to equal access to institutions and networks, particularly to high-quality education. Inclusion and incorporation are imperatives. There is nothing inevitable about the segregation of African Americans, the marginalization of Hispanics, and the fragmentation of American public education by race and ethnicity, and the mutually reinforcing processes of ethnoracial and socioeconomic stratification. The fundamental challenge of the next half century is uncoupling diversity and inequality.

CHAPTER 2

Toward a Connected Society

Danielle Allen

The United States is living through a major demographic transition that will surely upend our earlier approaches to thinking about identity, community, and social relations.[1] The question of whether by, say, 2040, we will indeed live in an egalitarian majority-minority country, where no group is in the majority and where such inequalities as persist do not track ethnic or racial lines, depends on choices we make now.[2] If we make the wrong choices, we may find that a black / nonblack binary has reasserted itself and that racial privilege is as strong as ever. Yet the demographic opening of the present moment presents an opportunity to renew and even perhaps make good on this country's egalitarian commitments.

Why focus on equality to define our social goals? Democracies are built on the twin ideals of liberty and equality. Up until the early nineteenth century, and in the period of the founding of the United States, these ideals were understood to be mutually reinforcing, not in tension. Political contestation following the rise of communism and during the Cold War, however, collapsed the concept of equality into "economic equality," and generated a conventional view that liberty and equality are opposed.[3] But a growing body of work in political philosophy now seeks again to understand all of the different types of equality—moral, social, political, and economic—and to understand the relationships among them. This body of work, to which I have contributed, focuses on the centrality of political equality, or egalitarian empowerment, to human flourishing.[4] Representatives of this approach include Elizabeth Anderson, Amartya Sen, Philip Pettit, and Josiah Ober. This line of work prioritizes democracy as the only possible route to justice rather than expecting that philosophers can close the question of the content of justice. The prioritization of democracy, and of political participation and empowerment as a necessary part of a flourishing life, establishes political equality as a fundamental feature of a just democracy. In this essay, I seek to sketch a framework for just social relations in democracies characterized by demographic diversity, and I begin from the presumption that healthy social relations in that demographically diverse democracy will be egalitarian. Note, then, that what we seek as a core democratic aspiration is not social cohesion but egalitarianism.

As we move forward in new conditions of diversity, can we finally make good on this country's egalitarian commitments? An affirmative answer requires that we make the right policy and ethical choices now. Whether we do that depends on whether we are able to articulate the right ideals and then connect them to both an effective policy framework and a cultural transformation that will make those ideals, or at least their closest approximations, real. In the United States our thinking about democratic social relations was governed, in the twentieth century, first by ideals of assimilation and integration and then by a competing ideal of multiculturalism. In this essay, I argue that we should replace these with an ideal of "social connectedness." As an ideal, social connectedness denotes a society where bridging ties, across lines of difference, are formed at a high rate and where individuals themselves frequently participate in such bridging ties. I will describe this ideal in more detail further on, and explain its connection to egalitarianism and, in particular, political equality. But most important, achieving such an ideal requires both a revised framework for policy making and a project of cultural transformation. The purpose of this essay is agenda setting, and so at its end I will address the work that needs to be done to develop both a policy framework for social connectedness and a project of cultural transformation.

Older Ideals: Assimilation, Integration, and Multiculturalism

The ideal of social connectedness is an answer to the question of how to achieve a healthy, egalitarian, and democratic society in a context of great diversity. It will therefore be important to be explicit about the conceptual challenges posed by the idea of "diversity." These are best seen by scrutinizing specific institutional efforts to wrestle with the concept, but even before undertaking such scrutiny, we will find it useful to look back in history at our earlier ideals, to remind ourselves how earlier generations deployed the concepts of assimilation, integration, and identity in attempts to answer questions similar to our own. Although these earlier ideals have long been discredited in scholarly circles, they easily reemerge in lay conversations as individuals working inside of particular organizations seek to grapple with the topic of how to scaffold social relations in conditions of diversity. Hence, it is worth being clear about their content and consequences.

First, for assimilation. In the late nineteenth and early twentieth centuries, a "common schools" movement spread across the United States, broadening the reach of public schooling and by 1918 achieving compulsory education in all forty-eight states then in the union.[5] The purpose of this movement was not, as we might now imagine, to increase the population's level of educational attainment but instead to spread Americanization in the face of staggeringly high rates of immigration. The image of the "melting pot"—an America in which ethnic differences would be smelted and fused into an identifiably "American" synthesis—dates to 1908 and expressed a powerful ideal of assimilation.[6] As formal systems of Jim Crow segregation were dismantled in the 1950s and 1960s, the goal of achieving healthy social relations took on the added dimension of the need to integrate across race lines. These two ideas—integration and assimilation—defined discussions of social relations from the early twentieth century through the early civil rights movement. The authority of these ideals waned in the late twentieth century, but even as late as 1992, the eminent historian Arthur Schlesinger Jr. could still organize his analysis of the prospects for U.S. social life around them, and his treatment provides a good example of the core problem with these ideals. He wrote: "Assimilation and integration constitute a two-way street. Those who want to join America must be received and welcomed by those who already think they own America."[7]

Although Schlesinger argues for a "two-way street," he in fact describes a one-way transaction in which one group assimilates into a dominant culture and the second group has only to embrace the idea of that assimilation.[8] As many have said, the assimiliationist ideal converts majority cultural norms and styles into the standard to which all others, whatever their cultural background, must adhere. To the degree that members of minority groups assimilate to the cultural forms of the majority group, the cultural resources of their original traditions disappear. For instance, one expression of the assimilationist ideal experienced by one late twentieth-century immigrant to the United States— and reinforced even by medical advice—was the view that immigrant children should actively suppress their mother tongues in order to maximize their performance in English.[9]

The novelist Ralph Ellison articulated a counterideal in his 1952 National Book Award–winning novel *Invisible Man*:

> Whence all this passion to conformity anyway?—diversity is the word. Let man keep his many parts and you'll have no tyrant states. Why, if they follow this conformity business they'll end up forcing me, an invisible man, to become white, which is not a color but the lack of one. But seriously, and without snobbery, think of what the world would lose if that should happen. America is woven of many strands; I would recognize them and let it so remain.[10]

In place of the melting pot, Ellison evokes an image of the United States as a woven tapestry, with richly intricate patterns of difference. As a novelist, Ellison did not convert his embrace of diversity into formal policy proposals, but those who worked in his wake—drawing on any number of intellectual, artistic, and activist traditions that had made points similar to his—developed a politics of multiculturalism. Canada was a leading site, thanks to the work of the 1960s Royal Commission on Bilingualism and Biculturalism;[11] and the Canadian philosopher Charles

Taylor provided the groundbreaking philosophical expression of this ideal in his 1994 book *Multiculturalism: Examining the Politics of Recognition.*[12]

Yet the multicultural ideal, too, has come under critique, from both right and left. Some voices, primarily but not exclusively on the right, feared that multicultural policies were antithetical to social cohesion, generating instead, to quote Schlesinger again, "fragmentation, resegregation, and tribalization."[13] On the left, the cultural critic Homi Bhabha argued that the multiculturalist view dangerously essentializes culture, as if there are fixed boundaries between cultural groups, and, for each of us, an unchanging individual identity tethered to the cultural tradition into which each is born.[14] Bhabha made the case that cultural life is instead characterized by hybridity, or a constant evolution in how each of us represents our identity, fashioning that identity, as we do, in contexts of contestation, out of whatever materials are at hand, which may themselves have disparate historical and cultural sources.[15]

Bhabha's arguments have been extended through the work of feminists like Iris Young, who argues for the importance of "seriality" and "intersectionality" to the identity of any given individual.[16] Let me take myself as an example. I happen to be a black, mixed-race, professional woman who is a mother of two and also a lover of poetry. Each of these roles comes into greater salience in different contexts. When someone invokes the responsibilities of mothers, I stand as one in a long series of mothers who have been called to attention by social and cultural cues. This is true of all my roles, which, we might also say (modifying Young's terminology), I inhabit serially, one after another, in an unending sequence that is unpredictable in its ordering. Additionally, the intersections of these different roles can be complicated: my identities as a professional and as a mother are often in conflict with each other.

These approaches to the topic of personal identity underscore a challenge for any effort to think about democratic social relations in conditions of diversity. Our approach has significant consequences for what we presume about individual identity. The assimilationist approach assumes that we can shed traditions in which we've been raised without doing damage to ourselves. The multicultural approach does not provide adequate space for self-identifications and for engagement in culture as hybrid and contested. Any approach to democratic social relations that hopes to displace these two paradigms must do a better job of recognizing that both tradition and adaptation matter for personal identity and, on the basis of this recognition, provide a framework for supporting individuals' psychological, as well as their social, flourishing.

The long-running critiques of assimilation, of an ideal of integration tied to assimilation, and of multiculturalism have hit their mark, undermining these concepts' credibility. As they have fallen away, their place has been taken by Ellison's word *diversity*. Over the course of the past two decades, across the corporate sector, the educational sector, and the organizational sector of civil society, one after another institution, organization, or association has produced a "diversity statement."[17] But the concept of "diversity" is not in itself enough to provide a framework for understanding how best to pursue the egalitarian social relations that can sustain democracy in conditions of demographic diversity. To understand why not, and to understand the other conceptual tools we need in order to develop healthy democratic social relations, we must turn to the conceptual challenges posed to the concept of "diversity" by critics, as well as to the challenges implicit in the concept itself.

Diversity: A New Ideal?

In 1952, as we have seen, Ralph Ellison laid down a marker for how we ought to think about the multifarious nature of American society. "Diversity is the word," he wrote. In 1978 the U.S. Supreme Court, in its *Bakke* decision, adopted a diversity doctrine for jurisprudence, writing: "[I]t is not unlikely that, among the Framers, were many who would have applauded a reading of the Equal Protection Clause that states a principle of universal application and is responsive to the racial, ethnic, and cultural diversity of the Nation."[18] The Court reaffirmed the diversity doctrine in the 2003 case *Grutter v. Bollinger*, "endors[ing] Justice Powell's view that student body diversity is a compelling state interest."[19]

Yet there have been dissenters to this view, not only those who argue in favor of "color blindness" in all matters of public and institutional policy but also those who argue that the "diversity rationale" fails to provide a framework for addressing historical injustice. As an example of the former, take Chief Justice John Roberts, who in a 2007 Supreme Court opinion about a K–12 school integration plan wrote, "The way to stop discrimination on the basis of race is to stop discriminating on the basis of race."[20] Roberts points us toward an ideal future where racial and ethnic differences are of no account and argues that we can reach such a future only by acting in the present as if racial and ethnic categories are irrelevant to public and institutional policies.

As an example of the latter concern that the "diversity rationale" leaves us unequipped to address historical injustice, take the philosopher Lionel McPherson. He argues that "mainstream institutions of higher education have a distinctive moral responsibility to promote racial justice with respect to Black Americans."[21] His argument is that black Americans were subject to forms of injustice over many decades—not only slavery and formal segregation—but also inequities in the use of the GI Bill and, throughout the twentieth century, in the real estate market, with the result that black Americans have had less access to educational opportunity than whites, a form of injustice that requires rectification. Thus, he writes:

> If everyone suddenly had what distributive justice assigns them, questions of corrective justice would be rendered moot: ideal principles would indeed have been actualized. To acknowledge this, though, is not to accept the notion that we would do better to stop worrying about the racially unjust past and, instead, should aim in the present for distributive justice. . . . Distributive justice, in any event, will not be taking effect in the United States in the foreseeable future. Corrective justice has an important role in the meantime.[22]

In McPherson's argument, the language of diversity fails to come to grips with the problem of historical injustice. It is oriented to the present, and does not provide a justification for rectifying past wrongs.

Both of these objections to the employment of a diversity rationale in the context of educational institutions make a mistake about temporality. Roberts's suggestion is that the way to transform the facts of the present into a desirable future is by acting as if that future already exists. Yet we have no empirical ground for considering this a valid theory of change, and the strategy turns attention away from the question of what justice requires in the present, given the particular social facts that characterize the present.

McPherson's argument, too, introduces a problem about temporality. Indeed, questions of historical injustice are always plagued by such problems. While our civil law system rests on the idea that those who have been wronged ought to receive damages through civil suits, those suits depend on the idea that the damages are paid to precisely the individual who was wronged. Generalized arguments about historical injustice tend to separate the question of who specifically was wronged from the question of who exactly would receive the rectificatory form of compensation. But the more significant problem, in my view, with an argument that would set a focus on "historical injustice" above a focus on "diversity," is that this view brings with it the danger, actually, of a perpetuation of problems of injustice. In asking us to think about how in the present we should rectify past wrongs, it too dramatically shifts our attention from what should be our focus: how to build fair and just structures of opportunity in the present in the context of great demographic diversity.

The focus on historical injustice tends to draw our attention only to the question of relations between "black" and "white" citizens; it tends to lead us to focus on an analysis of mid-twentieth-century social structures. But our overwhelming responsibility now is to understand precisely how our opportunity structures function in a world where several states are already minority-majority states, where Latino/as, not African Americans, are the largest minority group, and where the whole country is already well on its way to becoming a majority-minority country.[23] This is not to say that historical questions and legacies are irrelevant. To the contrary, to understand how to change current patterns, we do need to understand historical origins. In some sense, the problem of wresting the future one wants out of the material of the present involves interrupting patterns of path dependence that can best be seen and understood only by considering history. For instance, to understand our current choices, we need to recognize that one possible outcome of the fork in the road we now confront is that we might make choices that reinscribe the older black/nonblack binary. So how do we build opportunity structures that do distribute opportunity fairly and justly throughout the population? How do we make choices that genuinely move us past the gravitationally powerful black/nonblack binary rather than merely pretending to take us beyond it by obscuring it? We cannot answer these questions by turning away from the present and orienting ourselves toward an imagined future, nor by focusing exclusively on a vanishing past. Instead, we must scrutinize the present so as to see our new possibilities while also identifying the gravitational pull of historical patterns and the forms of path dependence that we must interrupt. I agree with Ellison that "diversity" is a concept that can help us focus on the possibilities inherent in our present while also requiring us to be clear-eyed about path dependencies that must be overcome.

Yet for all the usefulness of the concept of diversity and its orientation of us toward realistic descriptions of our contemporary demographic situation, it also introduces some conceptual challenges in its own right. It's not clear, for instance, that it captures an ideal as distinct from a description of social facts.

The Conceptual Challenges of "Diversity"

What exactly does the term *diversity* mean? What conceptual challenges does it introduce? The diversity strategic plan from the University of California–Berkeley answers these questions succinctly:

> For UC Berkeley to fulfill its core public mission, it must embody the following three principles to guide its vision of the University: excellence, equity, and inclusion. . . . But what about diversity? Is it not a guiding principle as well? Diversity is not a principle. Diversity is a fact; either it exists or it does not. Diversity—in many forms—does exist at UC Berkeley. But it is the principles of equity and inclusion— rather than representation—that will cement UC Berkeley's excellence and continue to position it as the preeminent public university in the world.[24]

This diversity statement presents us with two questions, one explicit and the other implicit. The explicit question is this: is "diversity" a fact or a principle? The implicit question is this: how can any given institution ensure that "diversity" is fully leveraged for its potential benefits, rather than being a source of detrimental costs? Berkeley's statement answers this second, implicit question by making the case that the principles of excellence, equity, and inclusion form the necessary framework for tapping into diversity in support of Berkeley's core mission. Answering these two questions—the explicit one and the implicit one—will lead us to the material that we need in order to build a framework for thinking about egalitarian social relations in innovative ways.

First, then, for the question of whether "diversity" is a fact or a principle. Here the answer must vary from institution to institution. In the United States generally, demographic diversity is indeed a fact. It has been a feature of this country's makeup since the founding. The colonists themselves were a more diverse lot than is typically acknowledged, and there was of course also the diversity brought by the enslaved population and existing in the native population.[25] Subsequently, successive waves of immigration have brought peaks of demographic diversity, for instance at the end of the nineteenth century and again in the present. Some 160 languages are spoken by students in schools in both New York City and Los Angeles.[26] Never has the world seen a polity or citizenry so diversely constituted as is currently the case in the United States.

Yet despite the fact of this broad and unprecedented diversity, that same level of diversity does not necessarily appear in the millions of organizations—businesses, churches, organizations, and associations—that populate civil society. To the contrary, in many sectors we continue to observe a high rate of monoculture across organizations and institutions. Sundays are nearly as segregated as they ever were.[27] The professoriate continues to be a predominantly white group, even as student bodies around the country become more diverse year after year.[28] Despite all the efforts of elite institutions to diversify their student bodies, an institution such as Princeton University cannot claim to have the level of diversity that Berkeley and Stanford have, both of which now have student bodies that are majority-minority.[29] And even though the public universities of California, for instance, Berkeley and UCLA, do have high overall rates of diversity, that fact should not mask the very low participation rates of African Americans on those campuses. For instance, as of the fall of 2013, African Americans made up 2.8 percent of freshman enrollment at Berkeley and 3.8 percent of total enrollment at UCLA.[30] Additionally, there is the question that emerges routinely as to whether the categories I have used here to indicate diversity or the lack thereof are the right ones. One might also want to attend to diversity of religious background or political leanings, diversity of sexual orientation and gender status, or diversity of linguistic background or disability, and so on.

In other words, "diversity" now represents a fact about our national demographics. But the many institutions and organizations of civil society themselves reflect a remarkable array of demographic patterns, ranging from the monoculture of my own recent home institution (the Institute for Advanced Study, a largely white and male environment) to the imperfect diversity of UC Berkeley (a campus characterized by majority-minority diversity but also by the startling underrepresentation of African Americans), to the remarkable pluralism of a small college such as Amherst College in Massachusetts, where 45 percent of the students are from ethnic minority groups, and each major demographic group plays a significant role on campus. Given the diversity of the country at large, no institution can any longer come to be monocultural entirely through random processes. Methods of recruitment into participation will be guided by the principles that the organization chooses as its framework for thinking about the fact of national diversity and its own specific demographic situation, and these will yield distinctive patterns of diversity or the lack thereof inside those organizations. In short, diversity is a *fact* of our national demographic situation, but it may or may not be a fact of the membership of any particular organization, institution, or association. Whether it is will depend on the *principles* that each organization, institution, or association uses for organizing recruitment into membership and participation.

Berkeley, for instance, describes its principles for thinking about membership thus: "Diversity—in many forms—does exist at UC Berkeley. But it is the principles of equity and inclusion—rather than representation—that will cement UC Berkeley's excellence and continue to position it as the preeminent public university in the world."[31] In other words, Berkeley employs two principles in relationship to the facts of national and institutional diversity. First, the university affirms the compatibility of diversity with the achievement of its mission. In contrast to segregationist-era institutions, the university does not seek to roll back diversity. Second, the university judges whether its on-campus diversity is at the level it should be with reference to principles of "equity" and "inclusion," not "representation." In this model, the fact that the number of African Americans on the campus is not representative of the number of African Americans in the population is not in itself a problem. The low level of participation by African Americans would be judged a problem only if it arises either from a failure of equity or from practices of exclusion. This formulation therefore commits UC Berkeley to scrutinizing its practices of recruitment and admission, as well as its own campus practices for welcoming and supporting the success of students, to evaluate whether they genuinely meet standards of equity and inclusion.

The question of whether diversity is a fact or a principle leads to a clear answer that diversity in any given institution, or the lack thereof, emerges from that organization's approach to recruitment into membership and participation, and therefore from the principles that guide that approach. Diversity may be a fact in a given institution, but as such it rests on a foundation of principle. Organizations do, then, have choices to make about which principles will guide their approach to recruiting and enrolling members. The choices they make will determine whether their organizations are characterized by diversity. The quest to understand the conceptual challenges that emerge from thinking about "diversity" has thus led us to identify a critical location at which principles are relevant to shaping our demographic landscape. Principles shaping recruitment into membership or participation in institutions, organizations, and associations will have a big impact on the nature of the conditions within which any given institution pursues a project of egalitarian social relations.

The second conceptual challenge posed by diversity is, as we have seen, this: how can any given institution ensure that "diversity" is fully leveraged for its potential benefits, rather than being a source of detrimental costs? Berkeley's statement proposes the principles of excellence, equity, and inclusion as a framework for bringing diversity in line with Berkeley's core mission. Here the Berkeley statement leads us to an important point about the relationship between diversity and egalitarian social relations. The question of whether diversity can be leveraged for positive social and institutional outcomes depends on things people *do* in contexts of diversity. Those positive outcomes don't flow automatically from the fact of diversity itself.[32]

Are "excellence," "equity," and "inclusion" the right principles for producing, where appropriate, institutions that are not monocultural? Are they the right principles for leveraging diversity? Here I propose a prior principle: "social connectedness." The goal of social connectedness emerges directly, as we shall see, from a definition of justice that centers on the achievement of political equality, and can help us think about membership policies in organizations and institutions. It is also a principle that speaks to the question of the interactional habits that are necessary to leverage diversity so as to achieve excellence, equity, and inclusion. In the sections that follow, I will define social connectedness, describe its role in helping us transform policy frameworks, and explain its role in helping us toward projects of cultural transformation in the direction of a successful egalitarian democracy.

A Newer Ideal: Social Connectedness

As we have seen, the ideal of assimilation pursues social cohesion while sacrificing individuals' particular need for connection to their communities of origin. The ideal of multiculturalism valorizes connections to those communities of origin at the expense of both a reasonable account of identity and social bonds. In place of these ideals, I propose an ideal of "social connectedness" that would characterize a "connected society."[33]

Scholars of social capital distinguish among three kinds of social ties: bonding, bridging, and linking. Bonding ties are those (generally strong) connections that bind kin, close friends, and social similars to one another; bridging ties are those (generally weaker) ties that connect people across demographic cleavages (age, race, class, occupation, religion, and the like); and linking ties are the vertical connections between people at different levels of a status hierarchy, for instance, in the employment context.[34] Bridging ties are the hardest ones to come by. Bonding ties take care of themselves, really. They start with the family and radiate out. But bridging ties are a matter of social structure. Schools, the military, political bodies—these have typically been the institutions that bring people from different backgrounds together. A connected society is one that maximizes active—in the sense of alive and engaged—bridging ties. This generally takes the work of institutions.

Importantly, more connected societies—those that emphasize bridging ties—have been shown to be more egalitarian along multiple dimensions: health outcomes, educational outcomes, economic outcomes.[35] Consider the impact of connectedness on labor markets. Research shows, for instance, that the majority of people who get a new job through information passed through a social network have acquired that information not from a close connection but from a distant one.[36] In other words, bridging ties spread economic opportunity rather than letting it pool in insular subcommunities within a polity. This makes sense. One's closest connections share too much of one's world; they are a lot less likely to introduce new information. We all know this intuitively. Whenever we're trying to help a friend who has been single too long, we scratch our brains to think of a further removed social connection who might connect our friend to a whole new pool of possibilities. Perhaps that seems like a trivial example. But the most important egalitarian impacts of social connectivity flow from bridging ties and their impact on the diffusion of knowledge. Scholars working in the domain of network theory routinely invoke the epistemic benefits of bridging ties to explain why so many economic, political, educational, and health benefits flow from them.[37] To the degree that a society achieves greater levels of connectedness, and more equally empowers its members in economic, educational, and health domains, it builds the foundation of political equality.

Perhaps one of the most profound examples of a failure at the level of associational life in a democracy is the case of racial segregation in the United States. I do not refer to a historical phenomenon, for instance, a relic of the mid-twentieth century. Racial segregation continues to have a significant impact on American life in the present and has been pretty conclusively shown to be at the root of racial inequality along all dimensions: educational inequalities in terms of achievement gaps between white and African American students; inequality in distribution of wealth; inequality in terms of employment mobility; inequality in terms of health.[38] Modern segregation is different from the mid-twentieth-century kind, as Thomas Sugrue details in this volume. Both suburbs and middle- and upper-class urban areas are more ethnically mixed than they were thirty years ago. But socioeconomic segregation matters more now. And poor African Americans and Latino/as are now more likely to face hypersegregation—along dimensions of both class and race.

A study of segregation by a group of economists shows that social network effects have a great impact on the distribution of goods and resources, such that segregation can be a driver of group inequality, even in hypothetical quantitative models where groups begin with equivalent skill sets and opportunities.[39]

Why does segregation have such profound effects? Common sense points the way to an explanation, which research has confirmed. All you have to do is think about what flows through social networks. At the most basic level, a human social network is like a web of streams and rivulets through which language flows. As language flows it carries with it knowledge and skills. That knowledge can be of the sort we recognize in schools: knowledge about the world or history or politics or literature. Or it can be of a practical kind: which jobs are about to come open because someone is retiring; where a new factory is about to be built, bringing new opportunities to an area. This sort of information also flows with language along social networks.

Any individual has access to just as much knowledge, skill, and opportunity as his or her social network contains. And since knowledge, skill, and opportunity are power, isolation in itself reduces resources of fundamental importance to egalitarian empowerment.[40] Language itself is one of the easiest markers to use in assessing how relatively well connected or fragmented any political community is.[41]

Now I need to underscore that the point I am making here is not about race or ethnicity. It is about social experience for all people. Everyone is benefited by a rich social network and harmed by a relatively isolated or resource-impoverished social network.[42] The American case of racial segregation just happens to be an extreme example of a basic phenomenon that crosses all contexts, times, and places. More egalitarian societies, scholars have shown, are generally more connected societies, and connectivity is equalizing.[43]

Importantly, achieving a connected society does not require that individuals shed cultural specificity. Instead it requires that we scrutinize how institutions build social connections with a view to ensuring that there are multiple overlapping pathways connecting the full range of communities in a country to one another. The ideal of a connected society contrasts with an idea of integration-through-assimilation by orienting us toward becoming a community of communities. A connected society respects and protects bonding ties while also maximizing bridging ties.

A connected society is one in which people can enjoy the bonds of solidarity and community but are equally engaged in the "bridging" work of bringing diverse communities into positive relations while also individually forming personally valuable relationships across boundaries of difference. Importantly, in a connected society the boundaries among communities of solidarity are fluid, and the shape of those communities can be expected to change over time. By continuously maximizing bridging ties, a connected society ensures steadily shifting social boundaries; some bridging ties will, over time, become bonding ties. And as what were once bridging ties become bonding ties, the quest to build bridging ties must migrate to new lines of difference and division.

At the end of the previous section I asked: what principle or principles should guide us in thinking about recruitment into membership or partnership in businesses, organizations, associations, and institutions? And what principle or principles should guide us in shaping interactional practices in contexts of diversity such that participants can leverage diversity to achieve, for instance, excellence, equity, and inclusion? The answer I offer is that we need policy frameworks that help us achieve a connected society, defined as one that maximizes the formation of bridging ties, and cultural habits that help individuals flourish in enacting social connectedness. I turn next to a policy framework for a connected society.

Building a Connected Society: A Policy Framework

As I have said, my method for thinking about democratic social relations in conditions of diversity starts with the question of how best to achieve political equality. Let me further specify the content of that ideal. I define political equality as requiring not only core civil and political rights (to association and free speech, to voting, to serving on juries and in public office, and so on) but also egalitarian empowerment across critical domains, in particular the domains of education, health, and economic opportunity. As I have indicated earlier (and in the notes), extensive research in the social sciences suggests that increases in the prevalence of bridging ties within a given social context provide more egalitarian outcomes across these key domains. Consequently, achieving a connected society in contexts of diversity ought to help us to achieve egalitarian social relations and political equality and to avoid a society of hierarchy and domination produced by opportunity hoarding along lines of difference. What sort of policy framework can help us get to the desired egalitarian outcome?

First, I must address a basic issue. My focus on political equality will prompt questions about the relation between political status, economic resources, and the distribution of the latter, a topic addressed by Anthony Carnevale and Nicole Smith in this volume (see chapter 3). While there is, in fact, significant overlap between what I have elsewhere labeled an "egalitarian participatory democracy" view of justice and the Rawlsian distributive justice view, the two approaches handle distributive questions differently.

In the Rawlsian argument, the point of a theory of justice is to provide a framework that ensures that such material inequalities as exist are just. This approach has tended to lead to policies of redistribution (taxation and welfare, for instance). In the egalitarian participatory democracy argument, the purpose of frameworks for resource distribution is to support political equality or, broadly understood, egalitarian empowerment. To borrow Jacob Hacker's formulation, the "egalitarian participatory democracy" view effectively shifts the focus from redistribution to pre-distribution, and asks how we can build a set of social structures that do a better job of distributing resources in an egalitarian fashion in the first place.[44] This leads to somewhat different ways of formulating economic policy, as well as different prioritizations of the policy domains that matter for achieving just outcomes. As I've suggested above, the focus should be on those policy domains that affect the degree to which individuals have the opportunity to form bridging ties, and the rate at which the society as a whole is forming social ties. This means focusing on the following policy domains in particular: housing; transportation; education; labor markets; the structure of municipal and county-level administrative units; the structure of legislative districts at the state and federal levels; and so on. If we are to build a connected society, we need concentrated research on the question of which policy approaches to each of these areas would roll back current patterns of modern segregation and spur a more frequent formation of bridging ties.

In this essay, I can, at best, point to a starting point and to a handful of examples in the literature where the policy analysis rests on a recognition of the egalitarian consequence of bridging ties. For instance, Berkeley professor David Kirp points to the value of mixing rich and poor kids in preschool.[45] Michael Reich and Ken Jacobs, also at Berkeley, argue for local minimum wages where wage policies cover work performed in the area in order to tie wages to local living standards. This localism lifts wages without reducing jobs and refocuses employers on their obligations to those across class lines within their own communities.[46] Mixed-income housing is important as are other policies that seek to roll back or undo the effects of "exclusionary zoning, persistent red lining, selective withdrawal of public services, the segregation of low-income public housing, 'stop and frisk' policing concentrated in minority areas, school funding tied to property values and the political fragmentation of metropolitan areas."[47] Revised approaches to federalism and the overlapping structure of legislative districts could support an expanded education for citizens in the interest positions of others, as well as more equitable distribution of power to minorities and dissenters.[48] Elsewhere, I have argued that in the context of college admissions, we could increase the degree of bridging ties on college campuses, particularly elite campuses, by placing more emphasis on geographic diversity at the level of zip codes.[49]

This small set of examples is meant to be illustrative, not exhaustive, and simply to assist in making imaginable the points of intersection of the ideal of social connectedness with policy choices. Importantly, since the organizations of civil society formulate their approaches to recruitment, admission, and participation against the backdrop of society as a whole, broader questions of social structure also affect how membership and participation policies in institutions work in practice. Achieving a richness of potential for bridging ties in the membership of the organizations and institutions that populate U.S. civil society is as much a matter of a more broadly egalitarian background social structure as it is of the choices that particular institutions make.

In short, we need a new integrationism, and the novel resources found in work by scholars of network theory should permit us to bring fresh insight to bear on policy development. The specific policies of a new integrationism—one seeking to maximize the rate at which bridging ties are formed, a process that must constantly be refreshed as what were once bridging ties evolve into bonding ties—may well be very different from the policies of old integrationism. For instance, the pursuit of maximizing bridging ties somewhat shifts the focus away from a strict concern for proportional representation of all groups in all institutions. Yet clarifying the content of a new integrationism, based on network theory, is a project yet to be undertaken.

Building a Connected Society: A Cultural Framework

Pursuing the ideal of social connectedness and a world in which no group dominates any other cannot be accomplished through policy alone. There is just as much work to be done on the cultural front. Even if our policy frameworks help us more commonly build institutions that require, enable, or nudge us toward bridging ties, leveraging those ties for positive outcomes will depend on our having a deeper and richer understanding of the art of bridging. Just how much work is to be done can best be seen by revisiting some of the arguments in the "social capital" literature.

Over the past two decades, the idea of "social capital" has played an important role in the literature on democracy, diversity, and healthy or failing social relations. The scholarly literature encompasses multiple, and even conflicting, definitions of this term,[50] but work by Robert Putnam, particularly in his best-selling *Bowling Alone*, has come to define the landscape and shape policy terrain. In Putnam's formulations, "social capital" refers to the resources that individuals develop through their social networks, and the private and public payoffs that those networks bring. We gain jobs through social networks, but also well-being and happiness. These are private goods. As to public goods, our communities benefit from our social networks through their production of generalized trust, mutual support, cooperation, and institutional effectiveness.[51] In his analyses, social capital simply is what arises from certain kinds of interaction: volunteering, participating in political campaigns, attending block parties and neighborhood picnics, joining clubs like the Oddfellows and Rotary Club.

By virtue of focusing on declining participation in clubs like Rotary and the Jaycees in the 1970s and 1980s, Putnam traces a decline in "social capital" in the United States over the second half of the twentieth century. Notably, Putnam's research identifies social capital as what simply arises from certain facts on the ground—in particular, demographic homogeneity. Conversely, diversity inherently erodes social capital, as he argued in his influential 2006 Johan Skytte Prize Lecture.[52] In that lecture, Putnam made the case that there is a necessary "trade-off between diversity and community" that can, at best, be "ameliorated."[53] His proposed technique for ameliorating the trade-off between diversity and community is to reduce the salience of identity in people's lives.

In contrast to Putnam's empirical studies of what appear in his data to be erosions of social capital in diverse neighborhoods, complexity theorists and social psychologists have studied diversity in teams, both formally and empirically, and have come to the conclusion that diversity can and ought to strengthen the epistemological capacity of groups, but that achieving this depends on the group's developing successful modes of interaction.[54] In other words, social capital—and epistemological success in team contexts—are not things that simply emerge organically from demographic facts. Participants on a team, or in a community, have to have a body of knowledge—as well as skills and capacities—pertaining to social interaction if they are to succeed in the generation of social capital.

This helps us see an important lacuna in Putnam's argument. Our interactions with others in both structured activities (clubs, political parties, and so forth) and unstructured informal interactions are not unmediated, "natural," or somehow "essential" activities.[55] Instead, we bring to them expectations, capacities, competencies, skills, and knowledge (or the lack thereof) that generate the phenomena that emerge from our interactions: perhaps trust, perhaps distrust; perhaps a commitment to mutual benefit; perhaps an agreement to disagree and drift apart.[56] Structured activities—for instance, club membership—can help set expectations for participants and educate them in the competencies, skills, and knowledge that lead to interactions that generate "social capital."[57] Even informal, ostensibly "unstructured" interactions are mediated by protocols of engagement disseminated by local and national cultures. In this regard, the activities that Putnam sees as the source of social capital are perhaps better understood as clusters of rituals, rules, and protocols that mediate interaction in ways that do (or do not) generate "social capital." Once one sees those structured and unstructured social interactions in this way, one realizes that they can be broken down into: (a) the interactional contexts into which they invite participants, (b) the particular capacities they demand of participants, and (c) the capacities, skills, and knowledge that they cultivate in participants.[58] Seen in this light, specific activities like clubs, political parties, and recurring bridge games are no longer necessary to the production of social capital. Instead, what is necessary is capacities, knowledge, and skills that enable people to actualize the potential value of social relationships.

Another point follows from this recognition that "social capital" emerges not from any given activity itself but instead from capacities, skills, and knowledge applied to interaction in the contexts of particular activities. The capacities, skills, and knowledge activated by any given structured activity guide participants in interaction that will successfully generate social capital *in that particular social context*.[59] That is, if the relevant social organization has a very homogeneous membership (for instance, if all members are women of a certain race and class), then the body of knowledge captured and conveyed through the activity of participation in that organization will be very specific to the production of social capital in that sort of demographic and cultural context. What follows from this is the idea that capacities, skills, and knowledge relevant to producing the interactions that are most likely to generate social capital must vary with the social contexts in which they are supposed to operate. A further thought is that when bodies of knowledge developed in one social context are applied to a new social context, one should expect them to fail because of the mismatch.[60]

This helps explain an intriguing fact hidden beneath Putnam's presentation of his data in *Bowling Alone*. Putnam mentions the U.S. court system only once in *Bowling Alone*, a reference to the Supreme Court's 1896 decision in *Plessy v. Ferguson*. But in the period from 1954 to 1985, the period in which Putnam traces a major decline in participation in thirty-two face-to-face chapter-based associations, the U.S. legal system, at the level of the states, Congress, and the Supreme Court, rewrote the law of association, with very direct impacts on precisely the private clubs that Putnam analyzes. Most important were the legal changes and court decisions that made illegal the gender-exclusive membership policies of organizations like the Jaycees and Rotary Club. Importantly, those court cases followed developments at the state level moving in this direction, and these in turn followed citizen ideology away from gender-exclusive organizational forms. Not all of Putnam's thirty-two organizations were equally exposed to the legal changes, however; some were not affected by them because of protections for religious organizations or because their members were children. Whereas the median decline in membership for the whole set of thirty-two organizations over the period from 1970 to 1997 was 58 percent, the five organizations that were gender segregated but legally protected saw declines ranging only from 5 percent to 18 percent. What Putnam diagnoses as a decline in social capital is, I believe, simply a mismatch between old forms of social knowledge—not all of them, in fact, democratic—and changed institutional and organizational forms that demand more of us in a democratic and egalitarian direction.[61]

In other words, the organizations that suffered in the middle of the twentieth century were those whose historical cultures of interaction no longer aligned with the principles of membership they had now either chosen or been required to adopt. It is not diversity itself that is the problem in such an instance where something like "social cohesion" seems to be falling away. Rather, I suggest, the difficulty lies in a mismatch between historical interactional cultures and the new demographic facts of an institution.

If we begin to deploy policy frameworks that increase the frequency of the formation of bridging ties, and move us toward a connected society, we will need to support that policy work with cultural work that develops the interactional habits and practices to support success for all at actualizing the potential for value in bridging relationships. When an institution (for instance, UC Berkeley) articulates the principles that it wishes to use in order to ensure that the demographic diversity generated by its practices of recruitment is then leveraged to achieve its mission—in Berkeley's case, academic excellence—it is establishing the framework within which social practices must be constructed and social knowledge built such that members of its campus have the capacities, skills, and bodies of knowledge necessary to generate social capital in the context of the demographic circumstances of its campus. The same thing is true if we adopt the ideals of a connected society and of social connectedness for individuals. We will have to learn how to build an interactional culture that will help people succeed at social connectedness. The relevant capacities, skills, and knowledge are not merely technical or informational, but also include ethical content, as I have discussed in *Talking to Strangers*. They include knowledge not only about one-to-one interactions, or even group dynamics, but also about the material conditions that affect interaction: for instance, whether we have individual bathrooms or group gender-assigned bathrooms; whether a podium can be lowered to the height of shorter speakers or will always obscure their faces; and so on. What sort of interactional norms, capacities, skills, and knowledge do we need to cultivate inside institutions aspiring to support social connectedness? I seek to answer this question in the next section.

Capacities, Skills, and Knowledge for Social Connectedness

A "connected society" is one that maximizes bridging ties, and a "connected campus" would do the same. But bridging ties do not arise merely by virtue of assembling a group of people characterized by demographic diversity in a single location. Bridging ties emerge when individuals are able to interact successfully across boundaries of difference. They emerge when people have been able to convert an initially costly social relationship into one that brings mutual benefit.

I argued earlier that our social interactions with others are mediated by capacities, skills, and bodies of knowledge, which we can draw on to produce social capital in the specific contexts to which those capacities, skills, and bodies of knowledge pertain. To build a connected society, then, we need to identify the capacities, skills, and bodies of knowledge that constitute an "art of bridging," an art of forming productive social relationships across boundaries of difference. Certain categories of professionals routinely build valuable bridging ties: translators, interpreters, mediators, patient advocates, community organizers engaged with diverse populations, and members of global business teams.[62] Each of these groups of professionals has a tacit body of knowledge that might be tapped to flesh out the content of the art of bridging that requires cultivation in order for egalitarian social relations to arise in conditions of diversity.

To say that we need an art of bridging is not, however, to say that we can ignore the art of bonding. For the sake of healthy psychological development, all people need bonding relationships.[63] Bonding builds a sense of security and trust, supports for self-confidence that can, in the right contexts, undergird success.

A comprehensive 2008 study of student social life at UCLA, *The Diversity Challenge*, provides significant insight to the complex ways bonding and bridging intersect with one another. The study traces in-group and out-group friendships for the four major ethnic groups on the UCLA campus (black, Latino, Asian, and white) as well as participation in ethnic organizations and fraternities and sororities, which are functionally equivalent to ethnic organizations despite going by a different label. Students who come to campus having already had greater than average out-group contact continue in that direction, forming out-group friendships at far higher rates. Students of all ethnicities whose precollegiate experience has, in contrast, tended toward in-group bias (more positive feelings toward one's own group), anxiety about intercultural competence, and perceptions of discrimination are more likely to develop an extensively in-group friendship set. Yet the results of this proclivity to bond are different for different groups. On the negative side, this bonding further increases in-group bias, perceptions of discrimination, and interactional anxiety for all groups. Also on the negative side, for Latino/as at UCLA during the time of the study, those in-group bonding relationships led to lower motivation, attachment, and commitment. Yet for the Asians and blacks in the study these bonding experiences led to higher commitment, and for blacks they also led to greater attachment to the university and higher academic motivation, all indubitably good outcomes.[64]

These data dramatically make the point that not all bonding is the same and that there is much work to be done to understand (1) the mechanisms that generate bonding's positive effects, (2) the mechanisms that generate its negative (antibridging) effects, and (3) the mechanisms by which bonding itself might serve to teach people how to bridge rather than be insular.

The question of how we bond is deeply entangled with the question of whether we are able to bridge.[65] Again, not all bonding relationships are the same. We need to bond in ways that help to preserve the democracy of which we are a part.[66] Thus, the critical question for a democratic society is how we can bond with those who are like us so as to help us bridge with those who differ from us. In order for any method of bonding—for instance, that which begins from social homogeneity or interest affinity—to support our capacity to bridge, the very experience of bonding must cultivate receptivity toward the potential of participation in our bonding group by social dissimilars. I call this "cosmopolitan bonding." The question of just what sorts of styles and methods of social bonding can be cosmopolitan in this way is a difficult one, which I have addressed elsewhere.[67] Suffice it for our purposes simply to mark out the terrain by identifying this, too, as a core component of the capacities, skills, and knowledge necessary to build a connected society.

The important message, then, is this: everybody needs opportunities both to bond and to bridge, and everybody therefore needs the arts of both bonding and bridging. We also, importantly, need to learn ways of bonding that enable us to bridge. On college campuses, and in a variety of other social contexts, we need to give more attention to understanding and cultivating these two intertwined arts.

But here we come to an impasse. If our families and our therapists help us learn how to bond, who helps us learn how to bridge? There remains much research to be done—by sociologists, psychologists, anthropologists, historians, and philosophers—to deepen our understanding of the art of bridging, in order that we may more effectively cultivate it. For instance, we need research work that translates the insights developed in the business management literature (about diverse teams) and in the interpreter studies literature and scholarship about multilingualism (about communication) to a wider array of social contexts (schools, colleges, training programs, associations, political institutions, workplaces generally, neighborhoods, and so on). The work in the management literature rests on a foundation of social psychology, a foundation that ought to be updated with reference to the literature on stereotype threat. Moreover, the skills, capacities, and bodies of knowledge that make it possible to take advantage of diversity appear to be related to personality factors. In addition to social psychologists, we need to engage researchers whose focus is individual psychology on the question of how to scaffold forms of personality development that can support acquisition of the art of bridging. And last, we need to connect all these conversations to educational research. For the foreseeable future, a significant portion of our nation's children will be taught by people who have very different backgrounds from themselves. In order to maximize educational achievement, we need above all to learn how to train teachers to succeed in pedagogic relationships that operate in conditions of diversity.

By directing our attention toward an art of bridging, the ideal of social connectedness helps make imaginable the forms of human development necessary for cultivating egalitarian climates inside of our institutions and maximizing the benefit we draw from diversity. I must also underscore in closing, however, that new cultures of interaction are not themselves enough to achieve a connected society, if we do not also adopt a policy framework that increases the rate at which bridging ties can form. In other words, the cultural framework for social connectedness that I propose here requires as its necessary partner a policy framework for a connected society.

Conclusion

To return to the question with which I began this essay: will we, by 2040, live in an egalitarian majority-minority country where no group dominates any other and where such inequalities as persist do not track ethnic or racial lines? If we are going to achieve this, we need to recommit to an ideal of political equality, defined as egalitarian empowerment across the citizenry.[68] In order to ensure that political power and the other resources that support it (education, economic opportunity, health) are distributed in an egalitarian fashion, we need to maximize bridging ties. Unprecedented social diversity presents a challenge because it requires us to succeed in unprecedented ways in learning how to generate and support these ties. This requires policy and cultural work. We often forget that institutional and cultural work go hand in hand. We often want to know what laws we ought to change in order to achieve justice. Yet law does and should have limits, and beyond those limits, the responsibility to achieve our goals falls on our own shoulders. With regard to the latter, bridging ties must be activated—that is, made profitable for those participating in them—by individual people who have learned how to practice the art of "bridging." If we are to achieve a just democracy in conditions of unprecedented diversity, we need an egalitarian policy framework but also egalitarian forms of civic agency. Policy and cultural work must be pursued in tandem.

CHAPTER 3

The Economic Value of Diversity

Anthony Carnevale and Nicole Smith

In chapter 1, Thomas Sugrue lays the historical foundation for our subsequent discussion of our compelling interests. He examines the role of the 1960s civil rights movement in the systematic disassembling of Jim Crow laws, and provides compelling historical arguments detailing why separation and segregation persist today—new rules apply despite the 1960s uprisings and legislative changes. These unspoken rules reinforce racial and ethnic segregation first in urban and suburban neighborhoods, thus forming the predicate for racial and ethnic segregation in K–12 and postsecondary institutions. By extension, racial and ethnic segregation extends to the workplace—both in opportunities for employment and in access to high-paying, good jobs—and finally to prison populations, all owing to the impact of access to certain kinds of schools.

In chapter 2, Danielle Allen challenges the perception that racial majority is a sufficient condition to guarantee social cohesion and equity in a future America. She contests the view that social cohesion and equity, taken together, are sufficient to promote a "healthy, egalitarian, and democratic society in a context of great diversity." Indeed, she proposes replacing these constructs with a broader, more complex idea of social connectedness, which lays out ladders and lattices connecting the socially similar to broader societal and economic structures.

Both these essays and ours recognize the common thread of a changing demographic that will necessitate changes in the way we produce and distribute the factors of production. Where we diverge is in the definition of this change, which must both precede and result from these demographic evolutions. The following essay makes the economic case for diversity as necessary for the survival of an aging population whose production processes are dominated by skill-biased technological change.

Increasing diversity on college campuses is crucial in preparing people for work and maintaining the nation's economic competitiveness. To some extent, the need for a deeper appreciation of diversity on the job is purely a result of demographic change. Workers and customers are becoming more diverse and, at a minimum, individual employees need to accept diversity to avoid counterproductive conflicts. Ideally, employees need to value diversity in order to maximize the innovation that comes with diverse points of view. Moreover, an increasingly diverse customer base will be unwilling to do business with institutions that exclude them.

Anecdotal evidence, case studies, research in industrial organizations, and clinical findings in studies of group behavior tell us that diverse work groups are not only inevitable; they also can be more efficient, flexible, and creative at a time when the intensity and complexity of organizational life and economic competition reward these attributes the most. In the workplace, just as in academic settings, diverse groups discourage groupthink (a phenomenon where members of the group refrain from expressing and considering contradictory opinions to avoid upsetting group cohesion) and encourage more learning—the most critical asset in adapting to the speed of change in the new economy. Yet not all diversity results in net gains. Various counterarguments in conflict theory point to ethnocentrism and the difficult path to interracial trust in ethnically homogenous societies.[1]

One thing is sure: if we are going to *minimize* counterproductive tensions and *maximize* creative tensions that are inherent in a diverse workforce, we will need diverse campuses first. Already, almost six out of ten American workers require at least some college, and the number will grow as job skill requirements increase. Tomorrow's workers come from today's colleges, and the best way to ensure diversity in the workplace is to increase diversity on the campus.

Diversity in the Workplace and the Marketplace

There is more than demography at work in the growing economic importance of diversity on the job. There have been fundamental structural changes in the economy that, in combination, have increased both the volume of interactions among diverse workers and with diverse customers and the value of navigating these interactions successfully.[2] They include:

· The shift from an industrial economy to a postindustrial service economy
· An expansion in the terms of competition from the mass production of low-cost standardized goods and services to

competition based on quality, variety, customization, convenience, customer service, and continuous innovation
· The movement from mechanical modes of production to information technology

The growing volume and importance of social interaction among diverse workers and customers is a direct result of the structural shift from an industrial to a postindustrial service economy. As the new economy emerges, the roles of people at work are also changing. The shift from an industrial to a service economy results in an increasing share of jobs where human interactions are necessary to get the work done. As interaction among diverse workers and customers intensifies, failure to value diversity risks conflict and organizational failure.

In the new economy, both jobs and the skills they require are becoming more alike. There is a trend toward requiring skills that are hands-off, general, abstract, and personal, and applying those skills in the context of groups and nonrepetitive situations. In addition, the expansion in service functions in manufacturing and natural resource industries, in combination with the increasing dominance of the service sector, ensures that a growing proportion of employees need the broad, abstract, flexible skills typically required in service jobs.

The economic evidence of the shift from an industrial to a high-wage, high-skill postindustrial service economy is well established. A vast increase in productivity has allowed goods-producing employers to dramatically increase output without hiring more workers. Between 1967 and 2011, goods manufacturing in America almost quadrupled, increasing from $3,000 to $11,000 per worker in inflation-adjusted dollars. These huge productivity gains meant that employment in goods-producing industries remained flat, at 26 million, even as the overall U.S. workforce surged from 57 million workers in 1967 to 139 million in 2011. America created 82 million new jobs during those forty-four years, and almost all of them were in service industries.[3]

The increase in service jobs and the increased levels of human interaction it reflects result from the increased consumption of services over goods. With increasing wealth and productivity in goods-producing sectors, we have moved from the consumption of goods to the consumption of services—notably, health care, finance, computing, and education. In 1967, for example, 46 percent of consumer spending went to the basic necessities of food, drink, and clothing, goods whose production generally required low skill levels. By 2011, the more economical production of these goods meant that outlays on these basic necessities dropped to just 18 percent of overall consumer spending—a much smaller share of the pie than in 1967. While these slices have gotten smaller, the size of the pie has nearly quadrupled—going from $8,405 (in 2005 dollars) per person in 1967 to $32,713 in 2011.[4]

The shift to service jobs is driven not only by changes in what we produce but also by changes in how we produce it. The service industry content in the production of final output in every industry has increased dramatically. Overall, we are experiencing an increase in service functions and service jobs in all industries. Even the value-added networks that produce basic commodities such as food are a case in point: today, farmers account for only 5 percent of the value added in food production. Almost 20 percent of the value added in the food network comes from the bankers, insurance firms, advertisers, and other business services involved in bringing final food output to the kitchen table.[5]

What are we to make of this new postindustrial service economy? Many Americans are worried. They see an economy out of balance, with low-skill, low-paying, and dead-end service jobs replacing the good manufacturing jobs of the past. They wonder where the middle-class jobs of the future will come from.

And yet, at the same time that we have been hearing this narrative of national decline, the education level of America's workforce has skyrocketed. In the forty-four years between 1967 and 2011, the proportion of high school dropouts fell from 37 percent of adults to just 10 percent, while those with a four-year college degree or more rose from 13 percent to 32 percent. Looking at postsecondary education as a whole, those with at least some college went from one-quarter of adults to 61 percent of the workforce.[6]

This is a remarkable upgrading in the skills of America's workers. And demand is apparently high for these elevated levels of skill, as employers are paying substantially more for workers with postsecondary education. The college wage premium—the difference between the average wages of college- and high school–educated workers—has spiked since 1967. By 2011, that difference had reached 81 percent for men, compared to 37 percent in 1967. The story is similar for women, with the college wage premium rising from 54 to 81 percent over that period.

How does this picture of a service economy rich in high-skill, high-wage jobs jibe with the competing narrative of a declining manufacturing economy filled with low-skill, low-wage "McJobs"? The answer is that it doesn't. The shift in America's workforce has not been from factories to fast-food outlets. Rather, the key growth in U.S. employment has come in office and nonoffice settings like hospitals and schools that provide higher-skill services; nearly two-thirds of Americans now work in these higher-skill workplaces.

Successful interactions among diverse workers and customers have become more important as machines take on more of the repetitive manual and mental labor, and employees spend more time interacting with their peers and customers. The increasing capacity of machines to take on more rote tasks creates a parallel demand for flexible workers with a greater depth and breadth of technical skills to exploit the new information technologies. Work increasingly involves hands-off tasks, personal interaction with coworkers, and overlapping job responsibilities.

Modern information technology is ultimately biased in favor of higher levels of interaction among teams of highly skilled workers because it automates repetitive tasks but leaves nonrepetitive tasks and higher levels of human interaction to workers, who in turn need higher levels of cognitive and noncognitive competencies. Virtually all workers now have nonroutine interactions with one another face to face as well as through powerful and flexible information technology.

While this shift to high-skilled human interaction seems obvious in the growing service industries, it is also true in old-line industries like manufacturing. As technology subsumes hands-on tasks, manufacturing institutions shed direct labor. Fewer employees are involved in hands-on production, but more are dedicated to service functions peripheral to the production process. The challenge is no longer making the widget but rather figuring out how to design it, maintain quality, tailor it for various consumers, create state-of-the-art widgets quickly and conveniently, and come up with improved versions before competitors do. A similar shift to service tasks and activities has occurred on the factory floor. In manufacturing, for instance, the traditional team on the factory floor included a machinist, a maintenance person, a laborer, a materials handler, an assembler, and a supervisor. Today, one person working with more powerful automated technology has replaced all these employees. At the same time, this manufacturing technician has more responsibility for productivity, customization, quality, and speed not just at his or her assigned work station but also upstream and downstream in the work process. To operate beyond his or her work station, for example, the technician needs a new set of interpersonal and organizational skills. To cope with change and variety, he or she needs learning and problem-solving skills.

Business-to-business services, which employ highly educated workers, are the hidden hand transforming production and consumption recipes. Business services hold together the value-added chains in production and consumption networks. They include a variety of professional functions such as consulting, accounting, management, and legal services, as well as clerical services and finance.

The business services "supersector" has replaced manufacturing as the U.S. economy's largest industry cluster. That fact is the culmination of a remarkable reversal in fortunes. In 1967, manufacturing was responsible for 31 percent of all value added in the economy, while the business services sector accounted for just 12 percent. By 2011, manufacturing had declined to 16 percent and business services had jumped to 26 percent. The percentage decline in manufacturing almost exactly equaled the rise in business services.[7]

Widely distributed information technology allows the shift to complex human and organizational networks driven by widely shared information and direct consumer participation, making these new networks the dominant form of organization for both consumption and production in all industries. As the new economy emerges, work structures are converging on a common institutional format of interdependent work teams and organizational networks populated by diverse workers. Work teams, the smallest networks, are the basic building blocks of larger networks. The whole organization becomes a network of work teams. In turn, the organization is a member of a network made up of other organizations that are its suppliers, customers, regulators, and financial backers. Everything is interdependent. The rubber, steel, plastics, and electronics industries depend on auto sales; the banker depends on the health of the companies in the bank's portfolio.

As employees become more interdependent, social skills in diverse networks become more important. The technical knowledge necessary to perform a task must be accompanied by the more complex capability of assuming ever-changing roles in the context of diverse groups.

As the frequency of personal interaction with coworkers and customers increases, the ability to communicate in diverse work teams also becomes crucial. If individuals are to be effective in groups, they need good interpersonal, negotiation, and teamwork skills. Interpersonal skills include the ability to judge the appropriateness of behavior and to cope with undesirable behavior, stress, and ambiguity. Negotiation skills include the ability to manage and defuse potentially harmful disagreements in groups and institutional networks. Teamwork skills include the ability to cope with and understand the value of team members' different work styles, cultures, and personalities and to provide and accept feedback constructively.

As work becomes more of a social process, the ability to influence a diverse array of coworkers also becomes more important. Each organization is a bastion of implicit and explicit power structures. To be effective inside the organization, the employee needs to understand both. Without this understanding, leadership skills are misplaced. They can even be counterproductive if they become barriers to strategic organizational goals or positive change processes.

Networks are a crucible for learning in the economy and tend to increase entry-level skill requirements and lifelong learning requirements at all levels of the workforce. Workers need not only greater knowledge to get their jobs but also robust specific and general skills to continue learning on the job. Both institutions and workers now rush to keep up with and get ahead of consumer demand.

In the postindustrial era, learning and innovation have become more diffused in work teams and in production and service networks. The industrial era was driven by major inventions brought to market by firms like General Electric, General Motors, IBM, Kodak, and Xerox. Although bringing inventions to market is still characteristic of many industries—pharmaceuticals and chemicals, for example—postindustrial expansion is notable for using existing science and technology in ever more complicated learning networks. Google, for instance, creates new wealth by developing networks made from available technology in collaboration with its users.

Christopher Hill points to the rise of networked firms like Google, Federal Express, Walmart, and Amazon as examples of the growing reach of innovation beyond traditional research and development (R&D) to larger, often global, networks. He argues that these firms are fundamentally different from the industrial-era firms dominated by basic research. These newer networked organizations have learned to meet human needs in new ways without making advances in basic science. In his view, the cutting edge of technology-based economic innovation—and where the most value is added—is in making the interface with cultures, communities, and individuals more seamless and customizable.[8]

Available research shows that diversity has positive consequences for business outcomes in the postindustrial service economy. Research showing that racial, ethnic, and gender diversity is associated with better firm performance at the micro level and greater economic prosperity at the macro level is borne out by anecdotal evidence all around us. Cosmopolitan cities that benefit from the fusion of ideas and skills from different cultures tend to enjoy greater prosperity. Ager and Brückner, for instance, find that between 1870 and 1920, a period that saw a huge surge of immigration into this country, growing cultural fractionalization led to a significant increase in economic output.[9] Ottaviano and Peri observe a robust correlation between the increase in the share of foreign-born population and the growth in wages of U.S.-born citizens in various U.S. metropolitan areas between 1970 and 1990.[10] Similarly, Sparber finds that racial diversity enhances macroeconomic productivity of U.S. cities.[11] U.S. history is a testament to the economic value of the many immigrant groups that have made their home here and contributed to the country's prosperity.

The same dynamic holds true at the firm level. Herring analyzed data from the National Organizations Survey (NOS), a survey of business organizations across the United States, to

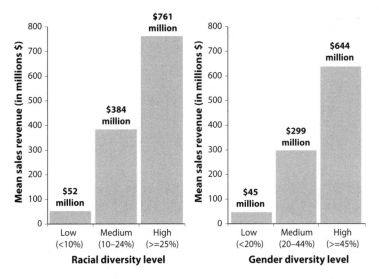

FIGURE 3.1. Racial and gender diversity is associated with higher sales revenue.

Sources: Cedric Herring, "Does Diversity Pay? Race, Gender, and the Business Case for Diversity," *American Sociological Review* 74 (2009): 208–224; and 1996–1997 National Organizations Survey (NOS) data.

show that racial and gender diversity is associated with increased sales revenue, more customers, a greater market share, and greater relative profits (see figures 3.1 and 3.2).[12] Firms with a high representation of women on boards of directors and in senior management positions demonstrate better financial performance than firms with few or no women in those positions.[13] Firms with greater gender and ethnic diversity have also been found to be more likely to innovate, to apply for more patents, and to have a greater breadth of patents in technological fields.[14] In an analysis of the banking industry, Orlando finds that cultural and racial diversity benefits firms and increases productivity, return on equity (ROE), and market performance.[15] Orlando,

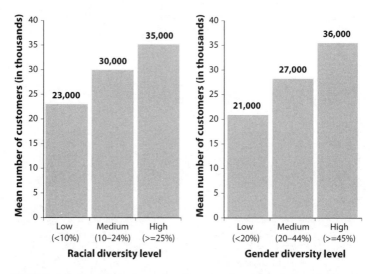

FIGURE 3.2. Racial and gender diversity is associated with having more customers

Sources: Herring, "Does Diversity Pay?"; and NOS data.

Murthi, and Ismail find a positive relationship between diversity and firm performance.[16]

In addition, Catalyst, a research and advisory firm, examined data on financial performance and representation of women in top management teams from 353 Fortune 500 companies and found that those with the highest representation of women in top management teams had a 35.1 percent higher ROE and a 34 percent higher total return to shareholders (TRS) than the group of companies with the lowest representation of women on top management teams.[17] In a separate analysis, Catalyst also found that among 520 Fortune 500 companies, those that were in the top quartile by representation of women on the boards of directors outperformed those in the bottom quartile, with a 53 percent higher ROE, a 42 percent higher return on sales (ROS), and a 66 percent higher return on invested capital (ROIC).[18]

Why should this be? Perhaps it's because diverse groups have a greater capacity for adept problem solving and effective decision making and are better at avoiding groupthink.[19] Hong and Page found that a diverse group of problem solvers randomly drawn from a large set of limited-ability problem solvers can actually outperform a group of high-ability problem solvers.[20] In his 2007 book *The Difference: How the Power of Diversity Creates Better Groups, Firms, Schools, and Societies*, Scott Page expands on this argument by explaining how diversity can have a strong positive impact within the right context. Attributes such as gender, race, and ethnicity shape human experience, he argues, which leads to the development of different perspectives on social issues, which, in turn, creates cognitive diversity. Such differences in perspectives, heuristics, and predictive models are highly beneficial for complex problem solving, and can even trump ability if the group of problem solvers is large enough, able enough, and drawn from a large pool of diverse problem solvers. Page attributes the wisdom of crowds, the use of open innovation methods, and the success of smart mobs to this type of diversity.

Context matters, however. A diverse workplace can be either a counterproductive source of tension or a spur to innovation. Cognitive diversity is beneficial for complex problem solving and predictive tasks, Page notes, but has few benefits for routine physical or cognitive tasks. For example, he argues, value diversity, which refers to differences in goals, preferences, and views, can be problematic when it leads to conflict about goals, although diversity is useful in coming up with various ways to accomplish an agreed-on goal.[21] Similarly, Jehn, Northcraft, and

Neale observe differences between what they call informational diversity and value diversity. In their classification, informational diversity refers to differences in knowledge bases, educational backgrounds, and perspectives, and they find that it benefits group performance. Value diversity, on the other hand, refers to differences in group members' views as to what the real mission, goal, target, or task of the group should be, and Jehn, Northcraft, and Neale find that it diminishes group performance and morale. Unlike Page, they do not distinguish between fundamental preferences and instrumental preferences, but their conceptualization of value diversity is in line with differences in fundamental preferences rather than instrumental preferences.[22]

Diverse perspectives can spring from many sources, including education, work and life experience, and personal identity. The extent to which identity differences correspond to relevant differences in problem-solving techniques is, of course, hard to measure empirically. But it stands to reason that, given their different life experiences, historical narratives, cultural and religious practices, and social positioning in American society, members of distinct racial groups cannot help but see problems differently and those differing perspectives should be of value. Cross-cultural evidence on academic papers supports this logic by showing that article impact and citations correlate with the coauthors' ethnic diversity.[23]

Cognitive diversity also can be shown to improve prediction and forecasting, a task that occupies a central role in the modern economy. Effective decisions about allocations of capital, venture capital investments, spending on research and development, and decisions to expand or contract all are dependent on accurate forecasting. Diverse predictive models (which again one would expect to be derived from different life experiences) improve collective prediction by reducing error correlation. For a group of predictors, their model diversity matters just as much as their average model accuracy. In fact, ensembles of diverse predictors constructed by computer and data scientists, using state-of-the-art machine learning classification procedures, outperform individual predictors by a substantial margin.[24]

It is only fair to note that the current state of diversity research is filled with inconclusive and conflicting findings. Page likens this situation to a bicycle test in which some children demonstrate measureable and substantial benefits of bike riding versus running, while those who have not learned how to ride a bike fall off very quickly. It would not be meaningful to compare the average speed of runners versus bikers in that context, but it would also be inaccurate to conclude that there are no advantages to bike riding. Indeed, the greater the skill in riding a bike, the greater the benefits from doing it. Likewise, Page argues, we are only in the early stages of learning how to maximize the benefits offered by diversity, and many organizations and groups do not apply or manage diversity effectively. Proper diversity management is what separates organizations that benefit from diversity from those that see no benefit or even losses to performance.[25]

So, what is proper diversity management? In their synthesis of the research, Roberge and Van Dick conclude that seven factors must be present: empathy, self-disclosure, good communication, group involvement, group trust, collective group identity, and a psychologically safe climate.[26] Wallace and Pillans point out other important elements for successful diversity management, including leadership commitment, an inclusive management style, a focus on performance and outcomes in assigning rewards and promotions, and the treatment of diversity as a business issue rather than a compliance issue. They also see value in addressing the problem of unconscious bias by tracking performance and promotion of minority groups and by helping minority groups understand internal company politics and informal networks. In the company at large, they argue, there should be mentorship and sponsorship opportunities for members of diverse groups, diversity awareness and behavioral training, setting specific diversity targets and measuring progress toward those targets, and flexible work arrangements that support the participation of women and other groups that may face challenges in meeting traditional employment and scheduling expectations.[27]

With proper diversity management, a diverse workforce also offers a better grasp of changing market dynamics: suppliers, contractors, and customers are becoming more diverse, too. As Robinson, Pfeffer, and Buccigrossi point out, people of color represent a significant emerging domestic market in the United States, with total buying power that more than doubled between 1990 and 2001.[28] Since 2000, the buying power of this group grew another 105 percent, reaching $1.9 trillion in 2013.[29] Along similar lines, Wallace and Pillans identify seven areas where diversity offers opportunities to organizations: it increases market opportunity for companies that are better able to grasp changing market dynamics of a more diverse consumer base; it increases stakeholder opportunity by satisfying demands for diversity from investors, suppliers, and clients; it gives companies access to a deeper and more multifaceted talent pool; it potentially lowers employee turnover, increasing financial opportunity; it increases public goodwill; it reduces the chance of legal claims related to diversity; and it increases regulatory opportunity, when taking a proactive approach to diversity helps avoid additional government regulation.[30]

Many analyses of the benefits of problem solving assume that problems and opportunities are simply features of a universal landscape, without stopping to consider that these perceptions depend on our interests, and that interests vary across identity groups. Changing demographics, then, means changing collective interests and a new set of problems. Decision making about which challenges to address in setting the economic, political, and social agenda will almost certainly benefit from input from diverse perspectives.

Developing germane perspectives and predictive models requires engagement. People with a rich array of backgrounds and experiences must be engaged at deep levels and must have incentives to construct new ways of thinking. Thus, the value of diversity will be contingent on how well we get along. The existence of the positive correlations described previously are all the more surprising in light of our lack of connectedness. Were we all able to construct dialogues across our differences, the benefits would be even larger.[31]

Education and the Training of a Diverse Workforce

Education is the weak link in translating America's demographic diversity into individual earnings and economic competitiveness.

The process by which intergenerational immobility by these markers persists seems to be very stratified. For example, at every level of education, differences in performance and outcomes by gender, but especially by race, ethnicity, class, and socioeconomic status, are characteristic of U.S. schools today, both K–12 and postsecondary institutions. In fact, racial school segregation in the K–12 system persists when schools are released from court oversight. Sean Reardon and his coauthors show that schools released from integration plans saw the gap between white and black enrollment grow by 24 percent after ten years as compared to schools still under court order.[32] The gap between white students and Hispanics grew by 10 percent after ten years. These racial and ethnic segregation patterns are often highly correlated with and indistinguishable from class and socioeconomic status. Coupled with these challenges, school districts in poor communities often receive lower allotments per student by the states and localities that fund them. The top 25 percent of school districts receive 16 percent more funds from state and local governments per student than the bottom 25 percent of school districts, according to data released by the Education Finance Statistics Center in March 2015.[33] Funding allotments have a significant impact on performance and outcomes by socioeconomic status and school district locations.

The postsecondary system mimics the racial inequality it inherits from the K–12 education system, and then magnifies and projects that inequality into the labor market and society at large. One way to measure the potential benefits of addressing racial/ethnic educational disparities is to consider how much of the pay gap between whites and African Americans/Hispanics is attributable to differences in educational attainment. We estimate that the racial/ethnic gaps in education cost the U.S. economy $278 billion and U.S. taxpayers $53 billion every year.[34] (We will return to this point in the section on policy recommendations at the end of this essay.) Though industrial growth is the true engine of opportunity underlying a strong economy that creates jobs, it is imperative that the workforce be prepared to capitalize on these opportunities. Moreover, as Autor explains, though most of the growth in income and prosperity accrued at the top of the income distribution, that growth is associated with higher education and cognitive ability.[35]

Higher education has not been able to keep up with the pace of upskilling in the movement from an industrial to a postindustrial service economy. Most jobs in the postindustrial service economy require at least some postsecondary education, and jobs in every economic sector are requiring higher levels of human interaction. Jobs increasingly require a mix of postsecondary skills, human interactions, flexible technologies, and the ability to work as a member of a team.

Since the early 1970s, the American economy has transformed from an industrial one, which featured more jobs for high school dropouts than for college graduates, to a postindustrial one, in which the share of jobs for dropouts now stands at only 11 percent. Consider, too, that in 1973 only 28 percent of prime-age workers had any postsecondary education. By 2010, that number had climbed to 59 percent. In fact, since 1973 the share of workers with an associate's degree, certificate, or some college has more than doubled—from 12 to 27 percent—while the percentage of workers with a bachelor's degree has risen from 9 to 21 percent. The percentage of workers with a graduate degree has increased from 7 to 11 percent over the same period. This trend will continue. By 2020, more than 65 percent of prime-age workers will need some type of postsecondary instruction. Roughly 30 percent will need an associate's degree, a certificate, or some college; 24 percent will need a bachelor's degree; and 11 percent will need a graduate degree. (See figure 3.3.)

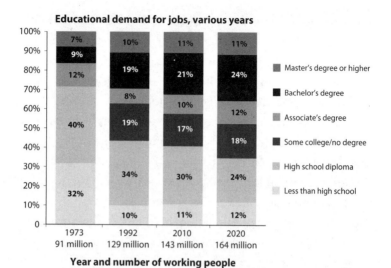

Educational demand for jobs, various years

Legend:
- Master's degree or higher
- Bachelor's degree
- Associate's degree
- Some college/no degree
- High school diploma
- Less than high school

Year and number of working people

	1973 91 million	1992 129 million	2010 143 million	2020 164 million

FIGURE 3.3. The shift from an industrial to a postindustrial service economy has made postsecondary education a core job requirement. Source: Anthony P. Carnevale and Nicole Smith, "Recovery: Job Growth and Education Requirements through 2020" (Georgetown University Center on Education and the Workforce, 2013). Percentages may not total 100 due to rounding.

Historical analysis shows that employer demand for college-level talent has been rising at about 3 percent per year since the early 1980s, while our education system has been increasing the production of college-level talent only by roughly 1 percent per year. This growing shortfall between our production of college talent and employer demand is the reason why the college wage premium over high school has spiked, as employers raise wages to chase scarce college talent.[36] Today (as noted earlier), college-educated workers in America make 80 percent more, on average, than workers without a college degree.

America could significantly reduce this wage gap by adding around twenty million college-educated workers to the workforce over the next fifteen years. (Right now, the United States is on track to add only about eight million.) Such an increase in the college-educated workforce would raise total output by $500 billion per year by 2025 (about 3.5 percent of GDP).

Though educational attainment levels of African Americans and Hispanics have increased over time, they still lag significantly behind that of whites. The growth rates of postsecondary attainment by race and ethnicity show tremendous progress since the 1980s, especially for African Americans (see figure 3.4). Since the initial postsecondary attainment rates for African Americans and Hispanics lagged far behind that of whites, however, people of color have a lot of catching up to do.

Economic gaps among diverse populations are a characteristic of the American economy. Differences in social, economic, racial, and political backgrounds are highly correlated with academic underachievement, lack of economic opportunity, poverty, and low social mobility.

Christopher Jencks, a professor of social policy at Harvard University, points out that the average black student scores between 70 and 80 percent of what white students score at the same age, starting in kindergarten and persisting even in college.[37] Furthermore, the racial wealth gap between whites and people of color is the highest it has been in twenty-five years: 2014 estimates by the Pew Research Center put the gap in net worth between African Americans and whites at 1,300 percent, and that between whites and Hispanics at 1,000 percent.[38]

Such enormous differences in achievement, attainment, wages, wealth, and opportunity cannot be easily explained. Parental income alone is not a sufficient indicator of the child's resources and success. Parents who follow "middle-class parenting practices" are more likely to increase a child's likelihood of success

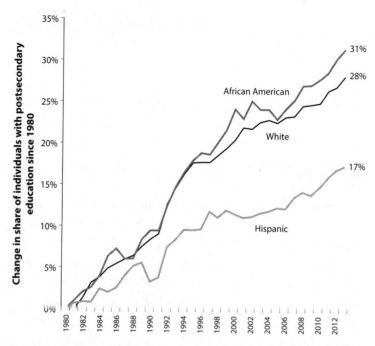

FIGURE 3.4. The growth rate of the share of individuals with postsecondary education has increased at a much slower rate for Hispanics than for African Americans and whites.

Source: Georgetown University Center on Education and the Workforce analysis of U.S. Census, *Current Population Survey*, 2013.

in school. But part of middle-class parenting practice is related to the parents' socioeconomic characteristics and background, and even the physical location of the home, and the effects of housing discrimination can last for generations: where a child lives today may be largely determined by where his or her grandparents were able to buy a house fifty years ago.

Nor is ability a sufficient explanation of the differences in success between the races. As Jencks and Phillips explain, "despite endless speculation, no one has found genetic evidence that blacks have less innate intellectual ability than whites."[39]

Coupled with relatively lower educational attainment, African American and Hispanic students are disproportionately channeled into less-selective open-access colleges and universities, and are more likely to obtain a subbaccalaureate credential as their terminal degree. African Americans' and Hispanics' access to postsecondary education over the past fifteen years is a good news/bad news story. The good news is that African Americans and Hispanics scored big gains in overall access to postsecondary education. The bad news is that both groups are losing ground in their move up to the most selective colleges relative to their growing population share.

Despite minorities' increasing access to postsecondary education, the system remains one of racially separate and unequal institutions. Polarization by race and ethnicity in the nation's postsecondary system reflects the racial and ethnic inequality in educational preparation it inherits from the K–12 system. These inequalities are then projected onto the labor market.

The absolute numbers of African Americans and Hispanics going on to postsecondary institutions has increased markedly and their share of enrollment in the top 468 colleges has increased slightly since the 1990s. But over the fourteen-year period from 1995 to 2009, 82 percent of new white freshman enrollments were at the 468 most selective four-year colleges, whereas 68 percent of new African American freshmen enrollments and 72 percent of new Hispanic enrollments were at open-access two- and four-year colleges (see figure 3.5).[40]

Race- and class-based inequalities in education overlap considerably, but race has a particularly negative effect on college

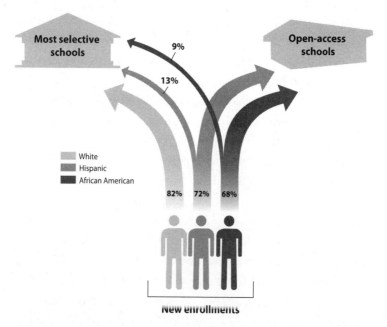

FIGURE 3.5. Between 1995 and 2009, 82 percent of new white freshman enrollments were at the 468 most selective four-year colleges, compared to 13 percent for Hispanics and 9 percent for African Americans. In contrast, 68 percent of new African American freshman enrollments and 72 percent of new Hispanic freshman enrollments were at open-access two- and four-year colleges.

Source: Anthony P. Carnevale and Jeff Strohl, "Separate and Unequal" (Georgetown University Center on Education and the Workforce, 2013).

and career opportunity. African Americans and Hispanics are especially vulnerable to class-based economic disadvantages because they are more highly concentrated in low-income groups and because they are more isolated both spatially and socially from the general society. Even as individual family income increases, African Americans and Hispanics usually remain concentrated in poorer neighborhoods. This in turn limits the positive effects of income increases, such as better schools. In short, race becomes a proxy for the negative effects of low-income status.[41] Hence, minorities are disproportionately harmed by increasing income inequality and do not benefit as much as whites from generational improvements in educational attainment or income growth. Although it is difficult to draw a line where racial discrimination ends and economic deprivation begins, the evidence is clear that both negatively affect educational and economic opportunity and are most powerful in combination.

The contribution of the polarized postsecondary education system to racial/ethnic educational disparities is revealed by the differences in outcomes among students who scored in the top half of their high school class on standardized college entrance exams (SAT or ACT), as seen in figure 3.6.

Simply expanding access to postsecondary education will not be enough to combat inequality. Currently, the U.S. postsecondary system is deeply divided between a top tier of roughly five hundred universities, which provide enormous advantages to their graduates, and the remainder of the schools, which confer far fewer advantages on theirs.

Students in the top-tier schools are disproportionately white and wealthy, and those top-tier schools spend two to five times more per student on instruction than other institutions.[42] The stark difference between the top tier and the rest can be seen in the graduation rates of minority students. The few African American and Hispanic students who attend the top-tier schools have a graduation rate of 73 percent, while just 40 percent of African American and Hispanic students who attend other institutions

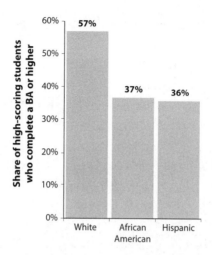

FIGURE 3.6. Among high-scoring students, 57 percent of whites earn a bachelor's degree or better compared with 37 percent of African Americans and 36 percent of Hispanics.

Source: Carnevale and Strohl, "Separate and Unequal" (Georgetown University Center on Education and the Workforce, 2013).

end up graduating. There are also huge differences in educational and career outcomes that separate all students at the top-tier universities from those at lower-tier schools.

Clearly, there needs to be a continuing push to broaden access for African Americans and Hispanics to the top-tier schools. Perhaps more important, however, America needs to invest much more heavily in the rest of our postsecondary institutions so that we can close the gap between the two tiers.

Implementing these policies will be neither cheap nor easy. But there are many precedents in American history for these sorts of investments: the founding of our land-grant colleges, the passage of the GI Bill, and the dramatic expansion of public universities in the postwar era. The legitimacy of such efforts is deeply rooted in the democratic project.

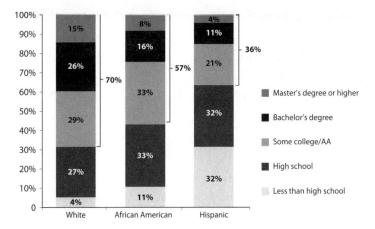

FIGURE 3.7. Only 36 percent of Hispanics and 57 percent of African Americans have some form of postsecondary education, compared to 70 percent of whites.

Source: Georgetown University Center on Education and the Workforce analysis of U.S. Census, *Current Population Survey*, 2013. The educational attainment presented is for prime-age (25–54) population. Percentages may not total 100 due to rounding.

For Hispanics, who represent the fastest-growing share of the labor force, the growth in postsecondary attainment has been substantially slower than for whites. From 1980 to 2013, the share of Hispanics with postsecondary education grew by only 17 percent. In comparison, the gain for whites during the same period was 28 percent, and for African Americans it was 31 percent. In 2013, slightly more than one-third of working-age Hispanics had some postsecondary education, compared to 57 percent of African Americans and 70 percent of whites (see figure 3.7).

Clearly, progress in raising educational attainment rates in the United States will substantially depend on improving educational outcomes for Hispanic and African American students, a population that has always presented a challenge for the postsecondary education system. For instance, the six-year completion rate at four-year institutions is 62.5 percent for white students, compared to 51.9 percent for Hispanics and 40.2 percent for African Americans.[43]

These disparate outcomes begin early. More than 60 percent of African American children and 35 percent of Hispanic children live with just one parent or with neither parent, compared with only 23 percent of white children.[44] By fourth grade, African American students are already 26 points behind their white counterparts in math and reading; Hispanic students are 19 points behind in math and 25 points behind in reading.[45] These students are also more likely to attend poorly performing secondary schools and to be subject to unequal disciplinary treatment.

As gaps in high school graduation rates and SAT scores show, students of color often continue to fall further behind their white peers throughout high school. The average freshman graduation rate is 71.4 percent for Hispanics and 66.1 percent for African Americans, compared with 83 percent for whites.[46] The average SAT scores of college-bound seniors in critical reading are 78 points lower for Hispanic students and 96 points lower for African American students; SAT math scores are 70 points lower for Hispanic students and 105 points lower for African American students; SAT writing scores are 73 points lower for Hispanic students and 97 points lower for African American students.[47]

These educational disparities also contribute to pay gaps between racial/ethnic groups. Hispanic men, who have the lowest educational attainment among racial/ethnic groups, earn 64 percent less than white men. Educational disparities are not the only source of pay gaps: women have a higher postsecondary

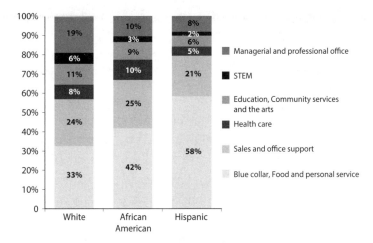

FIGURE 3.8. Across several occupational classes, African Americans and Hispanics, on average, have lower educational attainment levels than whites.

Source: Georgetown University Center on Education and the Workforce analysis of U.S. Census, *Current Population Survey*, 2013. The educational attainment presented is for prime-age (25–54) population. Percentages may not total 100 due to rounding.

education attainment rate (65 percent) than men (58 percent), but men's wages are still 27 percent higher.[48] Nonetheless, education is one of the main sources of socioeconomic inequalities in the United States.

The educational attainment levels of people of color significantly lag those of white workers across six broad categories of occupations. As shown in figure 3.8, Hispanic Americans are less likely to have postsecondary education and training than their white counterparts, especially in higher-paying occupations such as managerial and professional office and STEM (science, technology, engineering, and mathematics) occupations. More than half of prime-age Hispanics are employed in blue-collar, food, and personal service occupations, compared to 42 percent of African Americans and one-third of white workers (see figure 3.9). Overall, managerial and professional office and STEM occupations are much less prevalent among workers of color than they are among whites.

The pace of skill-biased technological change only intensifies this dynamic. Professional and technical occupations in health care services will experience the fastest growth through 2020, with a 31 percent increase in employment. Health care support, community services and arts, and STEM occupations will be the next fastest to grow, with a 26 percent increase in employment for each occupational category. As the U.S. economy slowly returns to normal in the aftermath of the Great Recession,[49] the key survival tools for workers will be accurate and timely information on where the jobs are and which industries will continue to experience high growth—and the education and skills required to do those jobs. Occupational segregation by race and ethnicity has clear consequences for wages and financial stability: managerial and professional office and STEM occupations earn twice as much on average as blue-collar, food, and personal service occupations.

Many of the patterns of occupational segregation and earnings disparities observed in the labor force start long before young adults enter their first job. These facts have significant consequences for wages in the marketplace. In postsecondary institutions across the country, women congregate in college majors that tend to command lower wages; minorities (except for Asian Americans) are underrepresented among STEM majors. For example, 36 percent of whites graduating with an associate's degree pursued degrees in relatively higher-paying STEM or health care professional and technical fields. This compares to

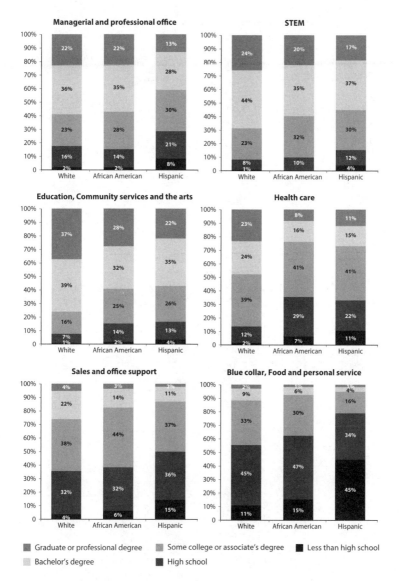

FIGURE 3.9. African Americans and Hispanics are disproportionately working in blue-collar, food, and personal service jobs. They are underrepresented in managerial and professional office and STEM jobs.

Source: Georgetown University Center on Education and the Workforce analysis of U.S. Census, *Current Population Survey*, 2013. The educational attainment presented is for prime-age (25–54) population. Percentages may not total 100 due to rounding.

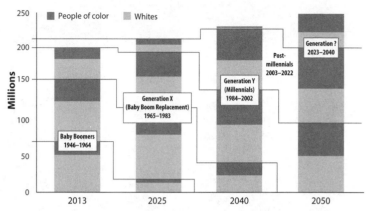

FIGURE 3.10. In the five generations displayed, the U.S. persons-of-color population is growing quickly.

Source: Georgetown University Center on Education and the Workforce and analysis of the U.S. Census Bureau Population Projections, 2015.

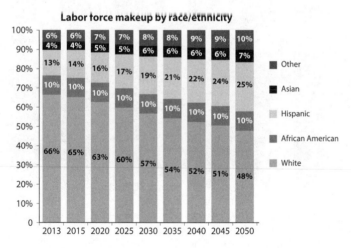

FIGURE 3.11. A changing population implies an equally changing labor force. By 2050, whites will no longer make up a majority of the labor force.

Source: Georgetown University Center on Education and the Workforce projection of labor force makeup by race/ethnicity, 2014. Percentages may not total 100 due to rounding.

32 percent of African Americans and only 26 percent of Hispanic Americans graduating with associate's degrees. Similar patterns hold for postsecondary vocational certificates and higher degrees.[50]

Educational inequality threatens competitiveness in our postindustrial future. The U.S. workforce is quickly becoming younger and more diverse. In 1980, 84 percent of all U.S. workers were white.[51] In 2013, it was 66 percent, and by 2050 whites will make up less than 50 percent of the U.S. workforce.[52] Every day, an estimated ten thousand baby boomers turn sixty-five, and by 2025 most of this predominantly white group of workers will exit the labor force.[53] As recently as 2013, a majority of the next wave of workers—those born between 1965 and 1983—were white as well. But future waves will be increasingly composed of people of color. (See figures 3.10 and 3.11.)

Summary and Conclusions

The goal of creating a diverse workforce—meaning increasing the number of women, racial and ethnic minorities, people from a variety of socioeconomic backgrounds, social classes, and countries of origin, as well as workers with varying physical abilities—has come to be accepted as a standard objective in corporate America. Various studies have attempted to evaluate the microeconomic impact of incorporating different levels of diversity into the organizational structure, with both positive and negative outcomes.[54] Results often depend on the way in which increasing diversity is actually implemented in the organization. For example, evaluation of the differences in economic outcomes among monolithic, plural, and multicultural organizations often concludes that multicultural organizations stand to benefit the most in terms of output and productivity.[55] From a macro perspective, many argue that the diversity in U.S. society has given us a decided competitive edge in securing direct investment, innovation, and creativity.[56] Yet despite the difficulty of putting an exact dollar figure on the value of diversity, it seems intuitively obvious that a diverse workforce in an increasingly diverse society is simply good business—increasing productivity, efficiency, competitiveness, and innovation.

Good intentions and sound business practices cannot overcome a history of social and economic segregation. Diversity viewed as a simple numbers game—where the token hire fills a quota—has failed to lead to true representation.[57] What's more, last hired/first fired policies take a disproportionate toll on minority employment when an economic boom turns into a bust.[58]

As the essays in this volume emphasize, the United States is undergoing a demographic transformation in which by 2050, for the first time in our nation's history, whites no longer will be a majority. Yet lagging educational attainment among minorities creates real concerns about how we will be able to meet the labor needs of the U.S. economy, much less maintain a workforce that reflects our society as a whole.

Over the past forty years, there has been a steadily growing disconnect between the need of employers for workers with postsecondary education and the ability of postsecondary institutions to produce those workers. The relationship between postsecondary education and career success strengthened dramatically in the 1980s, and today education and economic opportunity are more closely linked than ever. The recession that began in late 2007 accelerated this trend by eliminating many good jobs that required a high school education or less. Goldin and Katz have argued that these trends have led to substantial income growth for those with the wherewithal to get postsecondary education, and growing income inequality between them and those who lack such wherewithal.[59] Social policy analysts and commentators now rightly worry that the latter group will fall hopelessly behind in the twenty-first-century economy.[60]

In theory, the formula for success in American society rests on the notion that merit-based opportunity represents a just means for allocating social benefits—and wide access to postsecondary education means that anyone who is responsible and works hard can achieve career success. But this appealing theory does not take into account the underlying social structures that sort and rank students long before college admissions offices get involved.

In reality, merit and opportunity are powerfully influenced by circumstances of birth that give some children significant advantages over others. In a society where people start out in vastly unequal circumstances, educational achievement measured by test scores and grades can become a dodge—a way of legitimizing intergeneration transfer of wealth by rewarding the privileges that come from being born into a family with a comfortable bank account or of the "right" race or ethnicity.[61] We know that students with such intangible advantages go to college and graduate at much higher rates than equally qualified students from low-income families. The result is that American postsecondary education is becoming a dual system: the least advantaged half of the nation's students, most of them minorities, are concentrated in the least selective four-year institutions and community colleges, while their more affluent peers, most of them white, gravitate to more selective institutions.[62] But with demographic changes poised to make whites themselves a minority group by 2050, such a dual system is poorly equipped to create an educated labor pool that reflects its wider society.

What's more, economic and technological changes have spurred increasing demand for postsecondary education and training—and increased productivity from education, in turn, is creating economic growth. The fastest-growing occupations—such as STEM, health care, and managerial professions—demand workers with disproportionately higher education levels. About 28 percent of the increase in demand for postsecondary education comes from new occupations requiring postsecondary education or growth in occupations that already required high levels of education.[63]

The vast majority (72 percent) of the shift toward postsecondary requirements, however, comes from the demand for higher educational levels in occupations that previously did not require them. A foreman or manufacturing supervisor of the 1960s who may have had only a high school diploma has morphed into today's college-educated manufacturing engineer; the high school–educated insurance agent of the 1950s has become today's college-educated insurance broker or financial services advisor.

Our grandparents' high school economy, in short, has given way to the modern postsecondary economy. Postsecondary education and training is no longer just the preferred path to middle-class jobs—it is, increasingly, the *only* path.

There is a dark side to the postindustrial service economy, and it is getting darker. Our data reinforce a broader concern about growing inequality and declining income mobility, especially between education haves and have-nots. In theory, education is the preferred solution to growing inequality and declining economic mobility; in fact, it may be operating as an increasingly important mechanism for reinforcing the intergenerational reproduction of privilege.

The good news and bad news associated with the shift from an industrial to a postindustrial economy are intimately connected with the growing economic value of education. The college wage premium has more than doubled since the 1980s. The good news is that wages for college-educated workers have been increasing rapidly. The bad news is that this growing wage differential has contributed massively to the growth in earnings inequality since the 1980s, almost 70 percent of which is attributable to the increase in the college wage premium.[64]

Ultimately, the postindustrial service economy will be judged in part by its capacity for expanding choices for all workers and consumers. But so far the sweeping changes that come with the service economy have not benefited all workers or consumers. A substantial share of poorly educated youths and dislocated industrial workers have been left behind—a fact that many argue has become a drag on growth in the postindustrial economy.[65] There is credible evidence that inequality may have grown to the point where it is itself an impediment to growth.

There is also growing evidence that education has become an increasingly powerful gear wheel in the inequality machine. In the postindustrial service economy it is the complementarity between education and the access it provides to learning and state-of-the-art technology on the job that drives the cumulative differences in lifetime earnings. Young people born into families in the right neighborhoods with the best schools are best able to negotiate the pre-K–12 human capital development system and gain preferred access to postsecondary institutions and fields of study. That in turn puts them first in line for jobs.

The solution to the growing race and class inequity leads back to the venerable grand bargain implicit in the social contract of Western nations. In Europe in the eighteenth and early nineteenth centuries, the idea of democratic citizenship and a market economy grew together and were allied in their revolt against feudalism, but they were also natural antagonists: the abstract democratic ideal of equality clashed with the economic reality that inequality spurs productivity and entrepreneurship, which, left unchecked, creates lopsided accumulations of wealth. Widespread access to education, along with the expansion of social services from the welfare state, was meant to be the means of resolving these contradictions. The best summation of this school of thought was a speech given by Alfred Marshall to the Cambridge Reform Club in 1873, in which he proposed that expanding markets would pay for a constant expansion in publicly funded education and social services, assuring a democratic equality of opportunity that would, in theory, legitimize the inevitably unequal results. "The question," Marshall said, "is not whether all men will ultimately be equal—that they certainly will not—but whether progress may not go on steadily, if slowly, till, by occupation at least, every man is a gentleman" who values education and leisure more than the "mere increase in wages and material comfort."[66]

In 1949, T. H. Marshall (no relation to Alfred Marshall) refined that classic formulation in his argument for massive expansion in public education and the welfare state. He argued that the equality implicit in citizenship implied "a modicum of economic welfare and security" sufficient "to share to the full in the social heritage and to live the life of a civilized being according to the standards prevailing in the society." In his view, the institutions most closely connected with this notion of citizen equality "are the education system and the social services."[67]

As we struggle through the transition to the postindustrial service economy, the public ante required to maintain the social contract is going up again. We are overwhelmed by the public costs of maintaining our investments in the aging workers headed for retirement, expanding basic supports in health care and a livable wage for working families, and investing in the education of future workers.

In the United States, more than in Europe, education has always been favored over the more redistributive elements in the welfare state as a means of reconciling class differences and various forms of diversity. Americans have always relied on education as the gateway to opportunity because, in theory, it expands opportunity while maintaining the value of individual effort and responsibility. But in a society where people start out unequal, a two-tiered educational system makes "equality of opportunity" a cruel illusion.

Access to education does not guarantee social justice, but it does provide new possibilities for centrist policies that encourage political cooperation and social progress. The broad social consensus on the legitimacy of education as the arbiter of economic opportunity provides a starting point for dialogue. In fact, the belief that everyone should have an opportunity for a decent education is all that remains of common ground between reds and blues for addressing the structural inequalities that have emerged in this latest economic transition.

Policy Recommendations

Starting with the Great Recession of 2007–2009 and continuing with the political gridlock that led to across-the-board federal spending cuts in 2013, per capita spending on education by federal and state governments has been steadily declining—with a disproportionate impact on minorities. At a time when the global economy is increasingly competitive, this systematic disinvestment in the education of minorities poses the real risk that our children's generation will not possess the human capital to engage in the kind of innovation needed to stay competitive in the global market and contribute to economic prosperity at home.

In the short run, the rising demand for, and underproduction of, skilled college graduates has had positive repercussions—a persistent wage premium for college-educated workers. But for too many years, education expenditure on our nation's children has fallen as a share of overall spending. A recent study by the Urban Institute concludes that entitlement benefits for older Americans are increasingly crowding out expenditure on our nation's youth.[68] As federal stimulus dollars declined, many states have opted to continue funding programs for older citizens, who vote at higher rates than younger adults, at the expense of programs that benefit children.

Meanwhile, the number of retirees will increase from 40.2 million in 2010 to an estimated 88.5 million in 2050.[69] Given the impending retirement of baby boomers, we are facing serious shortages in our workforce.

In terms of sheer numbers, changing demographics will make matters worse: by 2050, new immigrants and their children are expected to account for 83 percent of the growth in the working-age population.[70] But will this emerging and ethnically diverse pool of workers have the necessary education and skills? Not if current trends continue. If we intend to meet our future workforce needs and take advantage of the vast human potential represented by this nation's changing demographics, we must reform current education and job-training investments to make sure that this generation is adequately prepared to take the reins we hand over.

Moreover, the class and race inequality in the postsecondary education system is especially daunting. It is much less likely now to spring from personal bigotry than from mechanisms that in theory are race- and class-neutral but in fact reliably produce unequal opportunity among classes and ethnic groups. The complexity and severity of these problems demand bold solutions.

Among all the ways to start out unequal, being born into the "wrong" race is still the worst. American racism persists even without racists. The lingering effects of Jim Crow still haunt our institutions, isolating minorities in ghetto neighborhoods and in decrepit schools that don't send kids to college. Race and economic class often go together, and poverty limits college opportunity among all racial and ethnic groups.[71]

Although affirmative action, both race- and class-based, seems clearly justified as a device to encourage race and class mobility and compensate for persistent racial and economic inequality, it is not clear that affirmative action as it has been known up to now gets at the roots of inequality. Whether it is race-based or class-based or a pragmatic combination of the two, affirmative action programs can help those who strive to overcome the odds, but they do relatively little to change the odds themselves. In the final analysis, disadvantage, like privilege, stems from a wide range of mutually reinforcing factors. That can be addressed only by policies with sufficient scope to match the complexity of the problem itself.

Because ethnic / racial education gaps cost the U.S. economy so much, reducing them could gain an additional $278 billion

per year for the economy. (This assumes earnings increases across the board, even though the increased supply of workers with bachelor's degrees will have the effect of narrowing the earnings gap between them and workers with high school diplomas.) Bringing all workers to the same educational attainment level that whites now have would increase productivity, narrow the pay gap, and increase job opportunities in occupations where minorities are currently underrepresented. The increased purchasing power that figure 3.12 represents would have a multiplier effect on the economy as a whole, raising the national GDP level. And although interventions required to address educational disparities may require substantial investments, the potential economic and social payoffs would be enormous, since workers with the lowest level of education benefit the most from improving their educational status.

Pointing out the increased inequality in the labor market due to the rising demand for skilled labor, James Heckman estimated that if we wanted to reduce wage inequality to 1979 levels—a year associated with low levels of equity distortions—it would require an aggregate investment in human capital of $1.67 trillion in 1989 dollars.[72] In 1998, this was considered a staggering cost, and in current dollars it would amount to just over $3 trillion. But even this figure is lower than the $4.75 trillion opportunity cost of racial/ethnic inequalities estimated by Belfield, Levin, and Rosen,[73] and it is substantially smaller than the estimated $11 trillion aggregate opportunity cost to the nation over the course of one generation.[74]

Transparency in the relationships between college curricula and potential wages can help students align postsecondary programs with upwardly mobile career paths. To tackle the

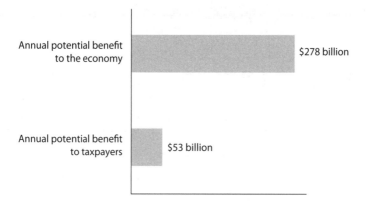

FIGURE 3.12. Racial/ethnic gaps in educational attainment cost the U.S. economy $278 billion per year.

Sources: Georgetown University Center on Education and the Workforce estimates of opportunity costs of racial/ethnic gaps in educational attainment using educational attainment from U.S. Census Bureau, *Current Population Survey*, March Supplement, 2013; and Anthony P. Carnevale, Stephen J. Rose, and Ban Cheah, "The College Payoff: Education, Occupations, Lifetime Earnings" (Georgetown University Center on Education and the Workforce, 2011). The annual opportunity cost is estimated based on an average forty-year career. The cost to taxpayers is calculated assuming an average tax rate of 19 percent.

inequalities that exist today, tomorrow's polices must address the biases and social pressures that affect the choices that people of color, women, and low-income students make regarding courses of study and occupations, which naturally have economic consequences. Among other things, this will likely require substantial changes to classroom culture and social stereotypes. It will also require colleges to provide greater transparency about the real-life financial value of different majors and courses of study. The value, expected payoff, and long-term costs of specific college majors and programs of study should be available to every potential and current college student.

The basic elements of a college and career information system already exist. At the federal level, the U.S. Department of Education's College Navigator system and the U.S. Department of Labor Statistics' Occupational Outlook Handbook are available to individuals interested in exploring their education and career options. At the state level, the State Longitudinal Data Systems, or SLDS, provides access to longitudinal databases and wage records data that already link education programs to workforce outcomes on a student-by-student basis. Coordinating these data would make it possible to show the earnings capacity of former students, linked all the way down to specific college courses. Better access to that information would allow everyone involved to make better cost-benefit analyses of particular degrees and programs of study.

Education and employment policy remain isolated in discrete silos of policy and practice. A new approach is needed to better connect postsecondary education and training, and to address the inefficient and inequitable use of education and workforce information. Such an approach would enable students to better understand how their postsecondary education and training options are likely to fit into the job market. It may also motivate institutions to be more accountable for shaping programs to fit students' needs and matching students to the requirements of the emerging global economy.

Education policy has been "access-centric" at the expense of "completion- and jobs-centric" in the past few decades. Changes in the methods of information dissemination on choice of education programs and employment possibilities are especially important for students of color and low-income students, who are disproportionately represented in open access, for-profit, and less selective colleges and universities—with decidedly lower completion rates. In many less selective institutions, students of color represent up to 40 percent of matriculation and graduation percentages. The war on access has largely been won, but we need to focus on where minority and low-income students go, as racial and ethnic segregation in the postsecondary system has economic consequences. Public policy that ties access to federal financing to the debt-income thresholds of college graduates should be advanced for all institutions as a prerequisite for access to the public purse.

We should provide high-quality universal early childhood education, with particular focus on children who historically have fallen victim to educational disparities. Early childhood education interventions are particularly likely to offer a high return on investment. For example, the High/Scope Perry Preschool Program for young low-income African American children produced a social return of $12.90 for every dollar invested in the program.[75] High-quality early childhood education is critical in giving children from disadvantaged backgrounds a chance to learn cognitive fundamentals and study habits that will serve them well throughout their educational and professional careers. The earlier a child receives proper education and care, the greater the chance of changing the odds of educational and career success for that child and the greater the benefits that will be recouped by society.[76]

A substantial body of research confirms the benefits of preschool education, finding both long- and short-term improvement in children receiving preschool education that can significantly affect the likelihood of their economic success. Heckman estimates that 50 percent of the variation in lifetime earnings is established by the time a person is eighteen years old.[77] Studies show that early childhood education develops critical soft skills such as cognitive learning, attention, motivation, and self-confidence, making it more likely for a child to succeed in school and in the workforce.[78] Overall, pre-K programs for disadvantaged children have a 7 to 10 percent annual rate of return, meaning that for every dollar a state spends on preschool, it will get back $60 to $300 from increased earnings and reduced dependency on public services over that child's lifetime.[79]

We should ensure more equitable assignment to K–12 schools, as well as more equitable distribution of resources among schools. Although the challenges of children from disadvantaged backgrounds start in early childhood, the K–12 schools are where these children clearly start to fall behind in educational performance. There are many challenges in K–12 education, from teacher quality to neighborhood safety, but two of the main factors that contribute to educational disparities (as discussed by Sugrue in chapter 1) are residential segregation and unequal distribution of resources among schools.

In the majority of the states, children are assigned to public schools based on where they live. In practical terms this seems to make sense: it makes it easier for parents to drop off and pick up their children, it shortens bus commutes, and it makes it easier for parents to participate in school activities. The serious unintended consequence, though, is that it creates racially and economically segregated and unequal schools based on local real estate values, with minorities concentrated in poorer neighborhoods and whites concentrated in more affluent ones. Thus, although schools have been legally integrated since *Brown v. Board of Education* (1954), de facto racial and economic segregation is as much a fact of life now as it was in 1954.

Since schools are financed by property taxes, schools that are relatively affluent to begin with—and which already have better-prepared students and more involved parents—also reap the benefits of the increased tax revenue that flows from higher local property values. Schools in poorer neighborhoods have the opposite problem: already struggling with the challenge of educating students who start out substantially behind and with less parental involvement, they also receive less money to grapple with these challenges. Advantaged schools get to hire the best teachers and counselors, provide the most up-to-date textbooks, and give their students access to the latest technology; schools in poor neighborhoods often have a hard time attracting teachers and counselors, supplying textbooks, or maintaining basic equipment.

Any school reform effort that fails to recognize or address this dynamic risks further aggravating the situation. For example, performance-based funding that does not account for student demographics can end up further depriving of resources those schools that face the greatest challenges. Teacher quality evaluations based on standardized tests can create further disincentives for good teachers to work in struggling schools in poor neighborhoods. School vouchers can result in the best students being pulled out of poorly performing schools, further segregating those students from those whose parents can't afford such options.

To address educational inequalities, K–12 educational reform efforts should address two important issues: school assignments that are not based solely on residence but do not put an undue commute burden on parents and students, and more equitable distribution of resources among schools in each state. Such efforts would begin to make progress toward realizing the ideal of equal opportunity in education.

We should support mentorship programs in high-risk schools and communities. While large-scale aspirational policies such as those discussed in the previous section await the right political environment, we should use whatever tools we have at our disposal to help young people from disadvantaged families. Mentorship is one such tool. Mentoring has been shown to promote positive behavior in young people, including higher educational goals and an increased likelihood of attending college.[80] Yet more than one-third of young people, including nine million at-risk youths, report never having a mentor while growing up.[81] Mentorship programs that target high-risk schools in poor neighborhoods are particularly likely to make a difference for at-risk students, who stand at the crossroads between high school and college graduation and eventual career success, on the one hand, and low-wage work or even crime, on the other.

We should expand college and career counseling in schools serving students of color and students from disadvantaged backgrounds. Students who study and do well in high school still have many important decisions to make that have significant consequences for their odds of completing a postsecondary credential and future career success. These include whether to pursue a bachelor's degree, an associate's degree, or a postsecondary certificate; whether to go to a four-year school, attend community college, or pursue an apprenticeship; whether to apply to a state flagship university, a highly selective nonprofit college, and / or an online program from a for-profit school; which major and occupation to pick; and whether or not to work or take on an internship while pursuing postsecondary education. These are complex questions even for education and workforce professionals to answer, yet many students have to make these choices with no knowledge or experience to guide them. Students from disadvantaged backgrounds often have no one in their family who has ever attended college who would be able to give them advice. College and career counseling is critical in helping these students make well-informed decisions and in supporting them through the college selection and financial aid application process. Yet many schools in poor neighborhoods do not have sufficient counseling staff. Whether through reallocation of funding that would allow these schools to hire more counselors or through community-based and online programs, high-quality evidence-based college and career counseling needs to be made available to as many students from disadvantaged backgrounds as possible.

Currently, postsecondary students often do not consider their careers until they complete their programs of study. By then it can be too late. American society invests enormous amounts of money and energy in the preparation, testing, and admissions processes that mark the transition from high school to a postsecondary experience, a period that spans only a few years in a person's life. Yet it invests very little in preparing that person for the great economic sorting that marks the transition from college to work, a process that will determine, in most cases, what that person will do after breakfast for the next forty-five years.

American society needs to pay attention to careers at the beginning of the postsecondary process, not at the end. Although it is true that people who choose majors or careers too soon tend to leave that field at a higher rate than those who choose later, the consequences for people who choose too late are more severe. Students who wait to the very end to make career decisions often experience the academic equivalent of buyer's remorse. The exposure or exploration model that allows a person to find his or her true talent and passion while in college is great—if the person can afford it. For everyone else, better decisions depend on better access to information that links training and education to careers.

This is especially true for adults who return to college and do not have time for exploration. For this group of working learners, decisions have to be timely and precise. Personal counseling, career counseling, comprehensive financial counseling, and basic information on how to navigate careers require access to social capital that many college students never get. The best way to relay this information to college students is through a counseling system at college. Many schools offer these types of "career ready," "career exploration," or "success after college" courses already, but they are often optional and, at best, arbitrary. We propose that this counseling system be information-based, available at the beginning of a person's education path, and mandatory for all college students.[82]

We should include students of color and low-income students served by higher education institutions in decisions affecting allocation of funding. In August 2013, the U.S. Department of Education announced that it would create a college rating program that scored colleges based on net price, the amount of debt students take on, graduation rates, and labor market performance of graduates, among other factors.[83] Metrics of access, such as the percentage of students receiving Pell Grants, were also being considered. The ratings scorecard released in September 2015 stopped short of including all of these variables in its template, however. Instead it gives the user a greater amount of control in coming to his or her own conclusions on college rankings by providing everyone with access to extensive federal data on student debt, school size, on-time graduation rates, and attendance-cost data, by institution.

Although in 2013 the Obama administration discussed possible legislation that incorporates his initial ratings schema into the allocation of financial aid funds by 2018, as of early 2016 no decisions on these statements have been put forward.[84] The new ratings, however, represent an important step toward ensuring that students get good value for one of the biggest investments they will make in their lives, and that society gets citizens who have received an education commensurate with actual educational spending.

Yet access should receive as much attention as quality and affordability in the new college ratings. Given our already polarized system of higher education, any policy affecting allocation of funding that does not adequately consider access—particularly, the share of students of color and low-income students served by each institution—could actually make things worse. It is important to ensure that the new rankings do not encourage colleges to cherry pick students even more than they currently do, as opposed to recruiting a diverse student body and working to bridge educational disparities.

PART TWO

COMMENTARIES

CHAPTER 4

The Diversity of Diversity

Kwame Anthony Appiah

Many of the questions that we now talk about under the rubric of diversity used to be discussed under other labels. There were cosmopolitanism, integration, and multiculturalism, as ideals; intergroup relations, caste, class, disability, ethnicity, gender, nationality, race, religion—or just plain "difference"—as topics; and bigotry, classism, racism, sexism, homophobia, and xenophobia, as vices to be combatted. The multiplicity of this list should remind us that both the kinds of diversity and the issues they raise are themselves quite various. So it's worth insisting that they are all appropriately connected by a single complex thread: that of the challenges posed and the rewards promised for us as individuals and as a nation by the fact of the great range of social identities in modern societies.

Societies were always significantly divided by gender. Complex societies, starting from the beginnings of settlement and the rise of agriculture, have always had status groups and internal divisions based on descent (caste, clan, ethnos, class) and on functional roles (farmer, priest, ruler, scholar, smith, warrior).

And human beings have always been prone to distinguish "us" from many "thems," both across the boundaries of groups that live together and within them. None of that, then, is new.

But three things, I think, are new about difference in the North Atlantic world in the period since the great late eighteenth-century revolutions against aristocracy, in France and the American colonies. One is the rise of a political and social ideal of equality that rejects the differential allocations of many goods in virtue of identity that were routine in the past. The initial challenge, of course, was to the distinction between the "higher" and the "lower" orders—between sans-culottes, bourgeoisie, and nobles, say, or the lower, middling, and upper classes.[1] But at the same time pressure began to build against inequalities on the basis of race (especially in the world created by the system of Atlantic slavery) and of religion—first challenging the divisions within Christendom, between Catholic and Protestant sects; then, a little later, challenging the divisions between Christians and Jews; and finally aiming for the inclusion of the full range of world religions now represented in all the societies of the North Atlantic, including even (as Bishop Berkeley put it in his *Treatise Concerning the Principles of Human Knowledge*) "the wretched sect of Atheists."[2] The idea was not the absurd one that we should treat everybody the same: it was rather that differential treatment had to be warranted by something, and that *these* distinctions—of gender, class, race, religion, and the like—did not, in themselves, warrant the differential allocation of social standing.

The second major change has been the proliferation of social identities associated with a massive increase in specialization in the economy, so that the range of professional identities and of forms of labor, and of groups associated with them, has exploded.

And the third change is that, although there have been multireligious and multiethnic societies since ancient times, modern patterns of migration, in the age after Europe's empires, have brought people together in multiethnic societies in which they are absorbed as individuals and not as groups. The Ottoman Empire was multicultural because it brought together Christians (of various denominations), Muslims, and Jews, as well as people of a variety of nationalities, such as the Armenians. But they were required to manage much of their own lives as communities. Now the Armenian American, like the American Christian, Muslim, or Jew, faces our state and society first of all as an individual. If you choose to respect the authority of a community or a priesthood—if you want to go to the rabbinical court for a divorce, or seek the dissolution of a marriage through an annulment in Rome—you may. But if you ask the government for a divorce, it will largely treat the matter as one between you and your spouse, not as one between a couple and a community. And, given that people of different identities can think about marriage differently, that may pose a challenge for the idea that the state addresses us each as the equal of all.

Now social identities such as the ones I have mentioned have two crucial things in common, despite the enormous variety of the criteria on the basis of which they are ascribed. First, all of them are associated with the fact that one can think of someone *as* (and treat them *as* and feel, both positively and negatively, about them *as*) a person of a certain social identity: we respond to people *as* men and *as* women, *as* Christians and Jews and Muslims, *as* lawyers and blue-collar workers, *as*

African American, white, Asian, and so on. And the second is that there are normative ideas in circulation—often contested, but effective nonetheless—about what it means to people themselves to have a certain identity, what it is to identify *as* a person of a certain kind, and what it means to identify someone else *as* a person of a particular social kind. How does race shape how blacks *should* treat each other or treat whites or Asians? How should men treat each other or treat women? There are contested claims everywhere about questions like these.

The fundamental point is that human responses—both cognitive and affective—are exquisitely sensitive to thoughts about ourselves and others *as* this or *as* that. This is one of the many ways in which we have evolved to be social creatures. Because of the central role of this phenomenon, let me give it a name: I'll call it "as-thinking." It is pervasive in both our conscious and our unconscious behavior.

Two pieces of recent psychological investigation can serve as representative of the way as-thinking can work below the threshold of conscious control. One is the exploration of what Claude Steele has called "stereotype threat."[3] We live in a society in which, at many points in our educational lives, we are required to take tests—PSAT, SAT, GRE, LSAT, MCAT—that can have a profound effect on our life prospects. It turns out that if you have an identity that is negatively stereotyped for what these tests are supposed to measure, simply thinking about your identity as you carry them out is likely to reduce your performance on them. Here is a summary of a typical experiment:

Asian-American girls ranging in age from kindergarten to 8th grade completed tasks that were intended to highlight their Asian identity, their female identity, or neither identity (control). Following these tasks, all girls completed items from a grade-appropriate standardized math test. Girls from lower-elementary and middle school grades showed a similar effect: math performance was bolstered when Asian identity had been made salient but harmed when female identity had been made salient.[4]

If we are trying to find out how good someone is at math, a test that displays her in a poor light when she's thinking of herself in one way and a good light when she thinks of herself in another doesn't do the job. Of course, the result here has consequences beyond the interpretation of test scores. If people perform badly at math away from the testing center when reminded that they are women, we should probably stop and think before reminding them; and we should also stop spreading the stereotypes that do the damage.

The second important phenomenon that has been studied recently is implicit bias. Here, once more, it is easiest to see what matters by considering representative experiments:

We developed a laboratory task in which participants made visual discriminations between guns and harmless objects (hand tools). A human face flashed just before each object appeared: a black face on some trials, a white face on others. . . . The task for participants was to ignore the faces and respond only to the objects.

When subjects were told to respond within a half second, "they falsely claimed to see a gun more often when the face was black than when it was white."[5] In another study, people tended to overestimate the proportion of time in a conversation taken up by women as opposed to men.[6] Our cognitive systems are tuned to respond unconsciously in ways that reflect social stereotypes—black men are dangerous, women talk too much—whatever our official conscious beliefs. African Americans, too, are susceptible to this "weapons bias." Women also tend to overestimate the proportion of time taken up by women in a conversation.

Phenomena like stereotype threat and implicit bias mean that many of the devices that we use to assign social rewards systematically fail to do what we claim for them. An SAT is meant to measure scholastic aptitude, not to discover losses in self-confidence caused by negative stereotypes or gains due to positive ones. Interviews are meant to identify people's job-related skills: if we're prone to think a woman who speaks as much as a man is talking too much, we can reject women whose performance in the interview is essentially the same as that of a man we accept.[7]

I have been talking about consequences of unconscious processes in which as-thinking plays a central role. But, of course, social life is full of *conscious* appeals to identity. The vast majority of men don't flirt with men . . . because they think of themselves and other men *as* men. Many rabbis would rather members of their congregations married Jews. Many employers don't want to hire transgender people. We accept more responsibility for the welfare of our fellow Americans than we do for political strangers.

With just these few examples before us, we can see that a plausible ideal of social equality doesn't require us to *ignore* social identities: rather, it requires us to take them into account only where they are actually relevant. So, if you have a staff full of white men, you may have a reason to hire a black person or a woman, provided your aim is to have a more diverse workforce. And one reason you might want to have a diverse workforce is that many modern forms of work involve creativity, and creativity requires a wide range of inputs, and people with different social identities—in part just because they have had different social experiences because of the pervasiveness of as-thinking—are likely to be able to make different contributions.[8] Another reason you might seek diversity is if you are investigating issues—such as racial or gender inequality—where people of different identities have different psychological "stakes." For a community of researchers with different stakes will likely be better at exploring all the options—for example, both the ones that leave those who are currently ahead exactly where they are and the ones that challenge their position—for reasons too obvious to be worth spelling out.

Remembering points like these is important because many people, having noticed the wide range of ways in which as-thinking leads people to treat other people unfairly, whether consciously or unconsciously, wrongly conclude that it is as-thinking in itself that is bad, rather than realizing that we need to analyze our appeals to—or our implicit attitudes toward—identities in particular contexts and see whether there is or is not a good reason for them. Because diversity is itself so diverse, such analyses can be difficult and often require us to take into account a wide range of considerations. But many of us start with the ideal that we should try to eliminate from social life as many of the unjustified appeals to identity as we can, even if we don't all agree about which appeals are in fact justified.

The essays in this volume show that we are further than many people realize from that ideal in cases where the lack of a suitable justification is not a matter of serious controversy. They also suggest some things that we can do about it. They focus on ethnoracial diversity because it poses some of the central challenges and offers some of the greatest opportunities of our American society. Thomas Sugrue (chapter 1) summarizes the evidence that we are still a society in which ethnoracial differences generate indefensible forms of inequality in education, income, and wealth. Anthony Carnevale and Nicole Smith (chapter 3) detail the persisting inequalities, especially in higher education, and argue that they impose a heavy economic cost in lost productivity, so that our economy would be stronger if we adopted a stronger commitment to the inclusion of African Americans and Hispanics in the best of our colleges and universities. And Danielle Allen (chapter 2) articulates an ideal of a connected society in which social policy in general, and educational policy in particular, aims to strengthen the bridges across ethnoracial identity groups. The lessons they all draw for ethnoracial groups also support greater inclusion across class lines.

I would like to suggest that it's worth reflecting on what conclusions we might want to draw about the importance of religious connection (bridging across religious groups) and political connection (bridging across political identities), especially in education, whose pivotal role in facing the challenges of diversity is rightly at the heart of each of these three essays. Outside the university, the evidence is that interfaith bonding and bridging in America is one of our success stories—as David Campbell and Robert Putnam argued in *American Grace*. On the side of our failures, I am not alone in believing that a kind of political segregation is one of the sources of the difficulties our society now faces in achieving effective policies on many topics, for this is one thesis of Thomas Mann and Norm Ornstein's *It's Worse Than It Looks*.[9] So I want to insist at the end, as I did at the start, that there are reasons for thinking about the many kinds of diversity together. If we are to make our colleges and universities

places where the necessary bridges are built across our diverse
identities, race, ethnicity, and class will be important for sure, but
so will disability, religion, gender, sexual orientation, and political
identity. Because the university is, above all, a place of intellectual
engagement, it is especially well placed to take up the challenges
of understanding and connecting the diverse kinds of diversity.

CHAPTER 5

Group Interactions in Building a Connected Society

Patricia Gurin

The essays in this volume raise fundamental questions for *Our Compelling Interests*: Will the rapidly rising demographic racial/ ethnic diversity brought about by immigration, differential birth rates among groups, and rapid aging of the white population result in growth, vitality, and social cohesion or stagnation and social fragmentation? Will the demographic diversification go on occurring with persisting racial/ethnic residential and school segregation, greater for some groups than others and in some locations more than others, and with income and wealth inequalities that have been increasing since the 1980s and are now greater than at any time since the 1930s? The authors concur that the choices and policies that we make now to decouple diversity and inequality will largely determine whether we will live in an "egalitarian majority-minority country, where no group is in the majority and where such inequalities as persist do not track ethnic and racial lines" (Danielle Allen, in chapter 2). Will the United

States invest now to ensure future economic competitiveness and "egalitarian social relations that can sustain democracy in conditions of demographic diversity" (Allen again)?

Although the authors of these essays vary in their estimations of whether the United States has the political will and governing capacity to make the needed policy choices and investments, they agree that foremost among the latter is greater investment in high-quality education, especially for the upcoming cohorts of the young who already are more racially and ethnically diverse than older Americans and who now disproportionately attend segregated and unequal educational institutions—from K–12 through college.

They emphasize the crucial role of higher education. I focus my comments on higher education as well, although of course the practices of other institutions must be analyzed for what reproduces segregation and inequalities, and what can and should produce the technical and problem-solving skills needed for future workers (Anthony Carnevale and Nicole Smith, in chapter 3), and produce the bridging mechanisms needed to create a connected society (Allen, in chapter 2). It is noteworthy, I believe, that these essays pay most attention to four-year higher educational institutions, especially highly selective ones, despite the likelihood that large numbers of nonwhite youths will obtain associate's degrees or certificates from community colleges or comprehensive four-year institutions. Moreover, a recent report by the W. T. Grant Foundation shows that occupational and earnings payoffs, though highest for a bachelor's degree, are greater for associate's degrees and completion of certificates than for obtaining merely "some college." Furthermore, "getting 'some college' from a four-year college will not confer a greater payoff than getting 'some college' from a two-year college."[1] The crucial issue is completing a degree—bachelor's, associate's, or certificate. Large investments must be made to increase the chances that racial/ethnic minorities and low-income students can attend and complete a degree in a four-year institution but also can attend and complete other postsecondary degrees and programs.

The Role of Group Interactions

What skills and capacities must all forms of higher education develop? Carnevale and Smith emphasize two sets of skills: information technical skills and problem-solving skills, both of which they say result from interaction among teams on complex tasks. Allen also emphasizes the importance of interaction—that institutions, higher education but also the military, political bodies, and civic organizations, must structure places and mechanisms that ensure successful modes of interaction across groups that are diverse on many dimensions and multiple identities. These interactions potentially connect people across demographic cleavages, enabling the creation of "multiple overlapping pathways connecting the full range of communities in a country to one another . . . toward becoming a community of communities."

Scott Page's work on diversity in two high-impact books demonstrates the importance of diversity itself and of interaction in accounting for when diversity produces robust outcomes.[2] Page posits that cognitive diversity in a group, which derives at least in part from the experiences and perspectives of people from different demographic backgrounds, produces more robust problem-solving outcomes than cognitive homogeneity. Along with the theoretical and mathematical support that

Page has provided for the value of diversity, empirical support has been found in studies of diverse and homogeneous decision-making groups. Members of the more diverse groups, compared to members of homogeneous groups, perceive the information available to them as more unique, and they spend more time on the tasks given to them.[3] Dissenters in diverse groups speak up more frequently than dissenters in homogenous groups, resulting it would seem in having more varied perspectives on the table in diverse groups.[4] But for these mechanisms to take place, people in diverse groups must actually interact and share ideas with one another. That doesn't necessarily happen just by putting diverse people in the same physical space.

Putnam's well-known research on the relationship between community diversity and the presence of social capital challenges the simplistic notion that diversity will automatically foster cross-group interactions.[5] He analyzed a survey, carried out with roughly thirty thousand individuals in both a nationwide representative sample and smaller samples representative of forty-one communities (census tracts) that varied greatly in their ethnic diversity. The results showed that residents of the most diverse communities "hunker down," more often distrust their neighbors, volunteer less, contribute less to charity, less often register to vote, and in all these ways exhibit less social capital than residents of the most homogeneous communities. What is especially relevant here is that residents in the most diverse communities, compared to those in the least diverse, withdrew from social interaction more frequently. His findings have been subjected to many empirical rebuttals[6] and theoretical critiques (see Allen, chapter 2). At the very least, however, Putnam's work clearly demonstrates that cross-group interaction is not an automatic consequence of diversity, and raises questions about when—under what conditions—diversity may result in increased social interaction and when it may not.

Turning to diversity in higher education, I have argued elsewhere that diversity should be looked at as just another institutional resource that can be used to achieve institutional goals.[7] In higher education institutions—community colleges, certificate programs, four-year colleges—diversity needs to be leveraged through the curriculum, research projects, university-community collaborations, and cocurricular activities so that diverse students actually interact with one another. That educational benefits are realized through planned efforts to improve the institutional climate and to promote interaction among diverse students is one of the best-established conclusions from research on diversity in higher education.[8] This point is echoed by Allen in distinguishing diversity as a demographic fact from what institutions (and individuals) do and should do in various contexts of diversity, noting that positive outcomes do not flow automatically from the fact of diversity itself.

Both frequency and quality of interaction are important. Frequent interaction across demographic differences has proved especially influential in accounting for students' learning from one another, engaging in complex thinking, and taking the perspectives of students from various different backgrounds.[9] But interaction can be both positive and negative, and have both positive and negative consequences. On the positive side, social psychological research indicates that cross-group interaction increases positive feelings toward members of other groups and reduces ethnic prejudice and intergroup bias.[10] A series of studies of roommates is especially illuminating because selectivity is controlled through random assignment of students to live together, a practice in place at many universities. (Most of these studies focus on the effects of having a cross-race roommate for white students because at the institutions where the studies have been conducted there are too few students of color to examine the impact on them of being randomly assigned another student of color or a white roommate.) Studies of white students who are randomly assigned roommates of the same or different racial backgrounds reveal a number of positive results. Unconscious prejudice and intergroup anxiety are reduced more among white students assigned a roommate of color than a white student like them, and they increased more than other white students in positive feelings toward members of other groups.[11] They also displayed greater comfort with minorities several years later.[12]

Not all effects in these roommate studies are positive, however. On the negative side, white students randomly assigned roommates of color, compared to those randomly assigned white roommates, spend less time with the roommate, have less involvement in shared activities, and feel themselves less compatible with the roommate.[13] A study specifically on emotions asked students, both white and of color, with cross- and same-race randomly assigned roommates to keep a daily accounting of emotions experienced with the roommate.[14] It showed fewer positive emotions, less felt intimacy, and fewer intimacy-enhancing behaviors (smiling, talking, appearing engaged and interested, warmth, ease in conversation, and pleasantness) among both whites with minority rather than white roommates, and among minorities with white rather than minority roommates.

Laboratory studies reveal negative consequences of cross-group interaction as well. Numerous studies indicate that intergroup interaction increases intergroup anxiety among both majority and minority group members, although continued intergroup interaction over time mutes some of these negative effects.[15] In particular, sustained intergroup interaction, which reduces the intergroup anxiety that is aroused initially, explains, at least partially, why intergroup contact reduces unconscious prejudice.[16]

These positive and negative consequences of cross-group interactions are important in themselves but they also set the stage for building trust, learning from the different experiences and perspectives of diverse students, and collaborating and solving problems together. Lest it seem that cross-group interactions should supersede interactions within demographic/identity groups, there is ample evidence in social psychological research that within-group interactions also produce positive outcomes, especially for mounting collective actions to redress injustice.[17]

Finally, other social psychological studies show that interaction across demographic groups may fail to achieve desired outcomes if differences in motivation for such interaction are ignored. Misunderstandings and differences in how people perceive, experience, and evaluate intergroup contact may occur as a result of differences in the societal privileges of the groups interacting with one another.[18] A series of studies shows that members of societally privileged groups prefer the intergroup interaction to focus on commonalities, while members of less privileged groups prefer it to focus on differences as well as commonalities.[19] Members of groups with societal privilege more often want to be liked in intergroup interaction, while members of groups with less privilege more often desire to be respected.[20] In explaining inequalities, members of privileged groups more often make system-justification and individualistic explanations, while members of less privileged groups more frequently make structural explanations for inequality.[21] Fear of being labeled prejudiced is more frequently expressed by members of privileged groups, while anger and resentment are more frequently expressed by the less privileged.[22] In terms of the goal of interaction, privileged group members more often advocate attitude change and prejudice reduction, while less privileged group members more often stress social change.[23] Unless these motivational differences and perceptions are dealt with, intergroup interaction may fail to achieve positive outcomes, and perhaps even reinforce or deepen negative ones.

These studies of processes that take place during cross-group interaction reveal the importance of structuring intergroup interactions not only to ensure diversity itself but also to create situations where interactions will be frequent, sustained, and facilitated to ensure engagement of members of all groups in communication, collaboration, and problem solving.[24]

Internal Diversity Structures and Interactions Promoting Bridge Building

In higher education institutions, some policies and practices promote internal social structures composed of students, faculty, and staff from diverse backgrounds. Often, it is expected that social structures that bring diverse people together will automatically result in positive outcomes. One example is random assignment of roommates, which we have seen may or may not foster positive relationships and learning across differences. Offering first-year seminars deliberately composed of diverse students with common interests is another connection practice, as is the increasingly used practice of project-based learning in which diverse teams and groups collaborate with one another. Merely putting diverse students into groups or teams does not, however, ensure productive interactions. Numerous studies demonstrate how racial/ethnic/gender dynamics from the wider society are often brought into groups and teams, thereby diminishing collaborative actions and problem solving.[25] A videotaped study of group presentations in an introductory engineering course reveals that women present more introductory material, summations, and conclusions, whereas men present more technical material.[26] (Men in that study also rated themselves and other men higher in leadership.) Groups and teams by themselves, without facilitation to equalize contributions from students of different demographic groups, will not necessarily produce learning across groups or less stereotyped assessments of skills and capacities.

Higher education institutions also use practices, perhaps unintentionally, that discourage interactions and connections across groups. Many institutions permit, and often promote, fraternities and sororities that are still largely composed of racially/ethnically homogenous groups. At my institution, residence halls vary in how much diversity exists through the practice of assigning students to various halls immediately when their housing applications are received. Because white students, especially the most affluent ones, disproportionately submit housing applications early, some residence halls and living-learning communities in them turn out to be less racially/ethnically diverse than other ones. The most striking practice that discourages diversity at my institution is using college GPA for eligibility for many interdisciplinary upper-level programs. Setting eligibility at high GPAs results, unintentionally, in a largely white composition of the undergraduate public policy program, the organizational studies program, the business school, and a program cutting across philosophy, economics, and political science. This internal GPA-based stratification reinforces the sorting of students by years of unequal education and shapes an unequal pathway to many postcollege internships and special opportunities. What needs to happen to ensure and leverage diversity for learning and democratic practice? One example is intergroup dialogue. I offer it because it is an example of what higher education institutions have done to create diverse learning situations that now exist in more than one hundred institutions and that have been extended to community-based work with youth,[27] and also because there is a large experimental study of its effects.

At most institutions, intergroup dialogue courses are credit-bearing and sustained across a full semester. Because students have to apply to enroll in these courses, it is possible to structure conditions that promote both frequency and quality of interaction. The courses comprise equal numbers of two (or more) social identity groups; cross-group interaction is sustained over time; the interactions are facilitated to deal with different motivations of participating groups and with both positive and negative processes; they contain traditional academic content focusing on intergroup histories and relations in the United States. Multiple dialogue courses are offered at many institutions, some focused on gender, others on race/ethnicity, sexual orientation, social class, and religion. The pedagogy of these courses involves discussion of readings and in-class active learning exercises designed to promote critical thinking skills, intergroup empathy, collaboration and problem solving, and communication skills of listening, inquiry, reflection, and sharing.[28] Its goals are to increase intergroup understanding, especially knowledge about historical and institutional sources of group-based inequalities;

building trust through positive intergroup relationships, especially intergroup empathy and motivation to bridge differences; and knowledge and practice of intergroup collaboration.

A large research project across nine universities with race and gender intergroup dialogue courses tested if these educational goals were achieved, and what processes accounted for effects. Applicants to gender- and race/ethnicity-based dialogue courses at these nine universities were randomly assigned either to the courses or to control groups. Random assignment was essential to ensure that effects that might be found could be attributed to participating in the courses and not to what might have happened for students just by being in college. Over a three-year period, 1,429 students were involved across 52 pairs of dialogue courses and control groups (26 pairs of race dialogue courses and control groups and 26 pairs of gender dialogue courses and control groups). All students were measured three times: at the beginning and end of a term when the dialogue courses were offered and again a year later. The effects of dialogue, evidenced by larger changes among the students randomly assigned to the courses than among students randomly assigned to the control groups, were demonstrated on twenty of twenty-four scales measuring intergroup understanding, positive intergroup relationships, intergroup collaboration, and both cognitive and affective processes generated by the dialogue pedagogy. Nearly all of these effects were still evident (though smaller) a year later, and causal modeling supported the theoretical framework guiding intergroup dialogue.[29]

Intergroup dialogue, and many other higher education examples, especially ones connecting diverse students, faculty, and staff with diverse communities in collaborative work, can produce the "bridging" Allen stresses.[30] They also relate to what Anthony

Appiah and Martha Nussbaum call a cosmopolitan education, one producing an outward orientation involving pluralistic perspectives, empathy, and critical thinking, and to what the Association of American Colleges and Universities and the Partnership for 21st Century Skills refer to as attitudes and skills students will need as leaders here and abroad, especially communication, collaboration, and problem solving with teams of people across cultural, geographic, and language boundaries within the United States and internationally.[31]

In conclusion, *Our Compelling Interests* has brought together incisive, different, but related analyses of intertwined social challenges of rapid diversification, continued racial/ethnic segregation, and increased economic inequalities, as well as critical discussion of choices and investments that need to be made to ensure a "connected society." In all of this, these essays point to the importance of policies and practices that ensure intergroup interaction, to which I add the importance of promoting positive bridge-building interactions across groups that can create a "community of communities."

CHAPTER 6

Diversity and Institutional Life:
Levels and Objects

Ira Katznelson

How should we appraise the meaning and prospects of diversity? How can we best capture the immense potential advantages of a layered human pluralism? What does fairness consist of in such circumstances? What kinds of social cohesion, within and across groups, are practically feasible and normatively appealing? These conundrums mark this volume's contributions, and thus invite sustained reflection about some of the most pressing issues for the future of the United States.

Barriers and Opportunities

To note the emergence of remarkable demographic heterogeneity does not, by itself, confer understanding or reveal implications of significance, possibility, or justice. Indeed, we are reminded that the seemingly simple historical category "white"—which was especially powerful in the eras of slavery and Jim Crow—itself has always been heterogeneous and internally racialized. In all, the very classifications we utilize to mark diversity, especially the idea of a racial majority (whether white or nonwhite), remain elusive. When, we might ask, should America's emerging new majority best be apprehended through the lens of color? (Latino, after all, is not a racial category, and the Latino population is racially diverse.) Most broadly, under what conditions should we be thinking in terms of the contemporary demographic categories as composing a majority and a minority inscribed by whiteness or its absence?

If we are at a point of inflection regarding matters of race and ethnicity in American life, especially as the growing and remarkably varied Latino population has been burgeoning to complicate the long-standing binary of black and white, and as patterns of amalgamation and separation have become more complex under conditions of increasing economic inequality and the shift from an industrial to a service economy that places education and skill at a premium, then it is imperative that we discern appropriate categories and standards for analysis and policy. The continuum of contemporary possibilities in fact is quite wide, perhaps wider than ever before in our history, ranging from a genuinely nondiscriminatory ethnic and racial order to renewed, very deep and hardwired, patterns of division inscribed by a combination of color and material standing.

In this context, it has become essential to consider which policy choices about institutional arrangements are possible that might tilt the balance positively under conditions of present uncertainty and, equally important, prevent deep inscriptions of color as the mark of opportunity. What, we might ask, are the barriers and opportunities for normatively desirable outcomes?

At the center of such considerations must lie what might be called an institutional imagination. Whether our focus is on education, neighborhoods, employment, civic life, political participation, or other zones of life, we can discern the crucial role played by institutions as congeries of rules and organizations that alter human probabilities. Institutions—including schools and firms; markets in labor, real estate, and finance; hospitals and concert halls; the churches and secular associations of civil society; political parties and armed forces; courts, legislatures, and government agencies—combine concepts, norms, organizational forms, and constellations of power. Each regulates participation and membership. Each establishes the likelihood of enclosure or boundary-crossing. Each, in short, organizes human possibilities, the prospects of connection and community, and the probabilities and meaning of choices about human attachments and the promise of pluralism.

The essays in this volume are significant contributions to our understanding of these matters. They advance a project concerned with comprehending how institutional arrangements deeply affect four distinctive levels of analysis: structures of diversity, experiences of living within a world that is demographically heterogeneous, dispositions different persons and groups bring to the interpretation of these experiences, and the variety of actions, including policy choices, that follow from these outlooks and understandings.

These descriptive, historical, and analytical essays thus offer vantages from which to interrogate such challenges, at once factual, analytical, and ethical. The questions that press on us are concerned with what exists, how it came to be, and, arguably most important, how a robust world of human difference and multiple bases of identity might be imagined and realized.

Within this situation, *diversity* is both appropriate as a cover word but also rather too general unless calibrated and specified more exactly in its analytical and normative dimensions as a category and rationale, each of which is a subject of contest and dispute among scholars and in public life. If we are to think creatively about these contests, attention to institutions and their configurations in conjunction with an analysis of ideas and interests is indispensable.

The authors understand that the remarkable demographic shifts under way in the United States that are transforming the color of the country's increasingly heterogeneous people—the results of global migration, legal changes, racial transformations, and new patterns of human connection—have meanings and possibilities that are not self-evident. Although the black-white binary continues, I would claim, to define the central line of division within the populace, it also is clear that a range of possibilities has been growing more open, more challenging, and both more promising and more perilous.

As the chapters in this volume identify the changing mix of peoples in American life, they distinguish important lags and barriers that must be surmounted if significant American institutions, notably including precollegiate and higher education, are to reflect and advance patterns of egalitarian diversity and social cohesion. These goals are not automatic results of a more varied population in terms of ethnicity, race, religion, and other markers of difference. The authors also look to a range of actions, such as more effective schooling and arrangements to promote human bonding, reduce disparities, and increase the likelihood of a rich and supple American pluralism.

The thoughts I offer do not take issue with the analyses and directionality of these sharply etched considerations and suggestions. Rather, I should like to emplace them within two intersecting frames. The first is defined by distinctive substantive domains (physical space, institutional security, material well-being, cultural regard, and civic membership). The second is characterized by analytical categories (structure, experience, dispositions, and action). Together, these typologies, I believe, can advance the goals of the essayists by helping to compose the elusive term *diversity* as an instrument of understanding and intervention.

Diversity's Domains

What is most at stake in the considerations we have been offered is the degree to which groups of citizens are connected to, effective within, or isolated from crucial institutional domains. The first of these concerns physical space. At one extreme, as in Jim Crow's formal structure, the central instrument of racial segregation was enforced institutional apartness, a physical absence or presence enforced by hierarchies of humiliation and control.

Not only in such stark systems of domination do such spatial-institutional patterns matter. More fluid social formations like those we experience today also are marked by terms of admission and exclusion. For black America, the arc of possibilities has considerably widened. Entry into mainstream institutions, remarkably including the presidency, is more open than ever before in American history. Simultaneously, however, various dimensions of de facto apartness, sometimes including total physical isolation, and including the distribution of children in public schooling, have deepened. And in today's increasingly complex demographic heterogeneity, categories of persons as broad as Asian and Latino (categories so large they are unknown as meaningful units of identity almost anywhere else) likewise are marked by institutional continua inscribed in physical space. Moreover, such matters are virtually never independent from dynamics of inequality. Separate but equal rarely shows its form, even when "separate" is the result of bonding choices within a minority group rather than the result of external imposition and constraint.

A second closely related zone of diversity and inequality is the security of persons, including their ability to move safely within and through various institutional locations unimpeded by markers of identity. In circumstances of unequal diversity, persons face harsh penalties if they seek to enter zones from which they are precluded or in which they are unwelcome. As targets of rejection, they may be threatened by both private and public degradation and violence. At the other pole of a continuum of possibilities, all persons are equally capable of traversing institutional domains irrespective of their color or identity.

Third is material well-being, the dimension of income and wealth that is attended to most often when diversity under conditions of inequality is considered. Presently, we can discern two notable, if familiar, trends. As the country's population has diversified in tandem with both deindustrialization and technological transformations, economic opportunities have sharply diminished for some, stagnated for most, and improved for a modest but well-rewarded minority. One result has been increasing gaps not just between but within groups sharing cultural, ethnic, and racial identities in ways that need to be more precisely specified. Such changes compel us to understand when and why inequalities grow and become more durable, and when they do not. More particularly, what role has higher education been playing in both reproducing and reducing different aspects of material inequality and mobility?

Cultural regard represents a fourth measure of diversity. Here, too, there is a spectrum that ranges from exclusion and silencing to a toleration of difference to warm inclusion marked by cultural syncretism. Of course, this domain is not independent of physical presence and security or material conditions. But it does have a significant degree of independence. In our universities, cultural regard is a recurring issue, independent of matters of admission, security, or impact on economic possibilities.

Last is the crucial province of civic membership. It is one thing to be present within an institutional realm, be it a country, a workplace, a neighborhood, or a university, and quite another to obtain meaningful civic capacity. A diverse institutional presence need not go hand in hand with the absence of visible or less perceptible barriers to effective influence.

Whether our emphasis is on higher education or on other central institutions, it behooves us to appraise diversity in each of these five lived sites. Specific situations are characterized by distinctive combinations, with each characterized by a continuum of possibilities, ranging from egalitarian connection to unequal isolation. Furthermore, particular institutional arrangements cross the frontiers of each of these sites, and thus it is important to consider the sometimes complex linkages that connect these elements of social reality.

Analytical Categories

In tackling such tasks, it is tempting to jump from situational structures to human agency, and, in turn, from agency to structure without fully attending to the connecting tissue offered by experiences and dispositions within distinctive institutions. In considering vexing issues generated by diversity, we tend to begin, not without good reason, with matters of social structure, including population. As examples, each essay in this volume opens with demographic information and a broadly shared observation that the United States is no longer predominantly white, nor simply divided between white and black; rather, they indicate, the country soon will be characterized by a majority of diverse persons of color.

Unless a good deal of specification follows, as Thomas Sugrue underscores, not very much follows from this accurate observation. Within the ambit of American life, perhaps the most challenging question lies in specifying the relationship between the country's new demography and its older, indeed foundational, distinction between white and black. Closely related is the issue of whether non–African American and nonwhite populations— ranging from Laotians to Chinese, from Koreans to Dominicans, from Salvadorans to Bengalis, and more—organize a coherent category to be contrasted with white Americans that makes a new numerical majority when joined to African Americans. If so, for which purposes and within which institutional domains?

Perhaps one way to address this issue would be to "split" rather than "lump" not only population groups but the domains of analysis I have identified. The meaning of color as a key aspect of diversity might well vary quite a lot from one set to another in the range of physical presence, security, material conditions, cultural regard, and civic membership. The descriptive, analytical, and policy challenges we thus face are daunting, for American society today is composed of assemblages of persons, identities, institutions, and possibilities more varied than at any previous time in the country's development.

What is most pressing are attempts to move beyond a thick accounting of structures toward appraisals of the middle ground of experience and disposition that lies between structure and human action. No individual and no group behaves simply as a result of its structural circumstances. Rather, persons experience structures in a double sense. They are shaped by structural arrangements within which they are located, and they gain experience of the institutions they inhabit together with impressions of those they cannot enter.

Neither do experiences directly lead to action. What I am calling dispositions—compounds of ideas and ideologies—always mediate between experience and behavior. This is true for elites who make policy, set institutional rules, and define zones of human possibility and for populations who have more limited capacities and who act to broaden how they can influence their lives.

Dispositions, too, are not immediately causal. As students of collective action long have understood, a disposition to act faces a good many inherent barriers, ranging from free-rider problems to repression. Within the policy arena, mechanisms that inhibit action include thick procedures and the hoarding of opportunities by those with the most to lose by changes to public affairs.

Toward Democratic Diversity

Making such distinctions can help treat diversity as both a substantive and analytical category. As few matters are more pressing, we need such templates not only to gain more precise understanding, but to appraise forms of institutional creativity and policy innovation. Which key mechanisms under conditions of ever-greater layered diversity can construct rich ties across groups and enhance access to such fundamental institutions as higher education? In what ways can network ties be arranged institutionally to maximize bridging without eliminating bonding, while addressing the dynamics of institutional access, structural barriers to connectedness, and differentials of power within and across groups? Which clusters of public decisions about education, the rectification of past harms, and social policy more broadly enhance prospects not just for a diverse, but a decently diverse, country? So doing, how should we appraise the relative weight played by race and ethnicity, on the one side, and the patterning of class, on the other? Within the economy, what is the relationship between the "empty places" of the job structure and the composition of the population to fill these places? Imagine an entirely nonracialized world, but one, like ours, in which economic inequalities of income and wealth are growing robustly. Would the latter produce a very different distribution than the racialized situation? More important, how should we think about the interconnections between economic trends directly linked to inequality in ethnic and racial terms and inequality driven by various market forces?

In all, we should be attuned especially to how decisions taken within and about institutional life advance or limit gains in the direction of what might be called democratic diversity, a pattern of inclusion that eliminates physical barriers, promotes human security, makes material conditions more equal, accords cultural regard, and is based on effectively equal civic membership. With artistry and rigor, we should aim at no less.

CHAPTER 7

Diversity as a Strategic Advantage: A Sociodemographic Perspective

Marta Tienda

Not in recorded history has there been a nation so demographically complex. So it falls to us, the American citizens of the 21st century, to fashion from this diversity, history's first world nation.

—Kenneth Prewitt

The historical record is replete with testimony about how diversity has challenged professed values of equality and inclusiveness.[1] After serving as director of the U.S. Census Bureau, Kenneth Prewitt acknowledged an underlying tension, however, which he posed as a question: "If diversity and discrimination have often been joined together in American history, will the pairing grow weaker or stronger—will racism and nativism wax or wane—as we grow more diverse?"[2] Collectively and individually the essays by Danielle Allen (chapter 2), Anthony Carnevale and Nicole Smith (chapter 3), and Thomas Sugrue (chapter 1) raise questions about the tolerable limits of inequality in a liberal democracy; about what must be equal for opportunity to be equal; and whether the national motto, E *pluribus unum*, is a chimerical aspiration undermined by what William Frey characterizes as "exploding diversity." Noting the rise in intermarriage rates, the proliferation of multiethnic places, and minority representation in public-office holding, Frey infers that civil rights legislation raised tolerance for diversity, and therefore he is rather optimistic about what the demographic narrative portends for integration and cohesion over the long term. I am less sanguine.

As the racial history of South Africa attests, group size neither confers power nor compels inclusion, even when formidable benefits are at stake. Sugrue's formulation of the diversity-equity paradox also tempers Frey's optimism about the nation's demographic destiny. Although I do not believe that diversity is inimical to social cohesion, for reasons elaborated below, I question whether the United States is on track to achieving what Sandra Day O'Connor described as "the larger national project of integration, a project that is at the core of twenty-first-century America's understanding of itself as democratically legitimate."[3] Like Daniel Lichter, I argue that the significance of diversity will depend on the human capital investments in young people.[4]

In a volume titled *Diversity and Its Discontents*, I cautioned that the United States was drifting away from commitments to broadly shared prosperity and social inclusion.[5] During the 1960s and 1970s, "it appeared that equal opportunity was a realistic goal; that social mobility and comfortable lifestyles were possible for all who put forth reasonable effort; and that both the War on Poverty and the civil rights movement would yield high social dividends toward the twin goals of reducing inequality and promoting racial and ethnic integration."[6] Following two decades of rising wage and income inequality, however, several legislative, statutory, and judicial decisions that signaled a gradual erosion of the social contract tempered my optimism about a shared commitment to a national project of integration.[7]

First, the Clinton administration passed the 1996 Personal Responsibility and Work Opportunity Reconciliation Act (PRWORA), which sought to curtail long-term dependence by imposing time limits on public assistance. In addition, by imposing a five-year moratorium on access to Medicaid and other means-tested income transfers, the welfare reform legislation redefined the terms of membership by drawing sharper lines between citizens and naturalized immigrants and legal permanent residents (LPRs). Second, the 1996 Illegal Immigration Reform and Immigrant Responsibility Act (IIRIRA) restricted states from granting in-state tuition to unauthorized immigrants. Although twenty states now offer in-state tuition to unauthorized immigrants, IIRIRA ignited a national debate about residency, legal status, and college access that continues to the present day.[8] Third, 1996 also was a turning point marking waning support for affirmative action: California voters passed Proposition 209, which amended the state constitution by prohibiting consideration of race in college admissions, and the Fifth Circuit Court banned the use of race in college admissions. The latter decision both challenged the 1978 *Bakke* opinion that recognized the educational value of campus diversity[9] and rekindled controversy about the merits of race-sensitive admission criteria that continues today.

That the rapid demographic diversification of the United States is occurring against the backdrop of persisting segregation, high levels of wage and wealth inequality, and stagnant social mobility challenges claims that the national project of integration is ineluctable.[10] For example, Richard Reeves notes that children born in the lowest quintile of the income distribution have a 40 percent chance of remaining there, but a meager chance—between 4 and 10 percent—of making it to the top.[11] These averages conceal even stronger immobility among population subgroups such as children raised by single mothers or black mothers.[12]

It is highly significant that what Frey characterizes as a "generational cultural gap" is grounded in social policies that inadvertently put the young at odds with seniors. This is not a new development but one whose consequences are dramatized by the diversification narrative.[13] In a prescient address to the Population Association of America in 1984, Samuel Preston identified an emergent paradox: although falling fertility should permit improvements in the well-being of children, the welfare of children declined as that of seniors improved, even as longevity at older ages increased.[14] In fact, since the mid-1980s, child poverty has remained well above that of seniors and, unlike that of seniors, has proven highly sensitive to macroeconomic conditions. After falling during the roaring 1990s, youth poverty rose gradually after 2001 and reached 22 percent in 2010—a rate comparable to that when Preston warned of diverging destinies among America's dependents.[15] Demographic factors, Preston notes, were involved in the unequal destinies of children and seniors, but changes in social policy figured prominently as well.

For several reasons, the economic underpinnings of this demographic development are highly consequential for the growing divide between the nation's dependents and for the national project of integration, but I highlight three that have important implications for public policy. First, entitlement programs for seniors—mostly Medicare and Social Security—are federally funded, whereas more than 60 percent of youth programs depend on state and local coffers.[16] This is significant for America's dependents because the federal government can run a deficit, which means that seniors are assured of their Social Security checks and health benefits. Because state and local governments must balance their budgets, education budgets were slashed during the Great Recession; less than half of states had restored their education budgets to prerecession levels by 2014.[17] Balancing budgets on the shoulders of future generations is bad public policy, and it will also affect future retirees.

Second, partly owing to soaring health costs and partly to changing demographics, the relative share of federal spending on youth has declined. In 1970, 7 percent of GDP was spent on health care compared with 18 percent in 2010.[18] Julia Isaacs and her associates show that domestic spending on children declined 23 percent between 1960 and 2010; during that period, spending on Social Security, Medicare, and Medicaid for seniors more than doubled.[19] According to the Center on Budget and Policy Priorities, Social Security and Medicare (excluding benefits for federal retirees) accounted for 40 percent of the 2014 federal budget; yet seniors represented only 14 percent of the U.S. population in that year.[20] That federal expenditures on children's health insurance programs (Medicaid and CHIP) require matching state funds further dilutes investments in young people not only because of large differences in state social safety nets, but also because restoration of spending cuts implemented during the Great Recession have not been fully restored in this area, either.[21]

Third, unlike seniors, who vote at relatively high rates, youths cannot vote before age eighteen; neither do they have an active political ally to lobby on behalf of their interests.[22] Initially established to serve retirees, AARP has become one of the most powerful lobbies protecting the interests of adults ages fifty and older.[23] There is no comparable omnibus organization serving youth, nor is there a social contract for youth comparable to Social Security for seniors. That education is mandatory and yet states are not mandated to endow all schools with equal resources[24] reveals an inherent flaw in the social contract for youth because it signals tolerance for inequality for the most vulnerable of America's dependents. In no small measure, Social Security shields seniors from income volatility over the business cycle. Investments in education and child health programs, by contrast, not only vary appreciably across states and localities but also have proved highly vulnerable to changing economic and political priorities. These circumstances render the emerging "generational gap" highly consequential for the future of the nation. The generational transition is essentially a policy gap, not a cultural gap, as Frey claims.

Population as a Strategic Resource

Like Frey, I see the unfolding diversification narrative as a *potential* source of strength, but one that is not guaranteed.[25] Notwithstanding rhetoric about pride in ethnic diversity and the innumerable contributions of immigrants to the nation's economic vitality, demography is not destiny; rather, destinies are shaped through policies that actively construct social bridges across groups and institutions, as Allen argues, or that exclude by default through benign neglect. The generational transition underway poses high stakes for the nation: rising global competition demands that the United States recommit to making human capital investments a policy priority in order to maintain its economic stature as a world leader. Unlike many members of the Organization for Economic Cooperation and Development (OECD), the United States has a population that is still growing, which is important for replenishing the labor force as the baby boom generation approaches retirement. As Carnevale and Smith note, more than ever before, maintaining a competitive edge in the world economy will depend more on the *quality* of labor than on the sheer quantity of workers. Human capital investments will determine whether American youth become highly productive workers capable of replenishing the Social Security coffers to support aging dependents while also bolstering innovation and economic growth. Although the United States retains first place as the largest economy based on nominal GDP, with a population four times as large, China is gaining ground and has already overtaken the United States based on purchasing power parity.[26]

There is an important historical lesson that can guide the future. Technological and military competition between the United States and the former Soviet Union compelled Congress to make massive investments in education, research, and defensive infrastructure. In addition to bolstering the economy, investments in education during the Cold War also ushered in a period of broadly shared prosperity by allowing the nation to harness a demographic dividend—a productivity boost garnered when college attainment rates of the outsized baby boom cohorts surged as fertility rates fell.[27] As figure 7.1 shows, the share of GNP spent on education spiked after World War II,

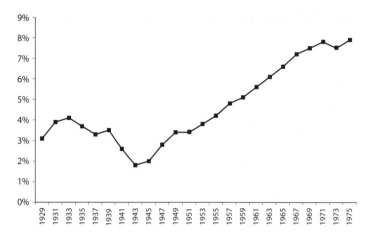

FIGURE 7.1. Expenditures for Education, as a Percentage of GNP
Source: Department of Health, Education, and Welfare, *Annual Report of the Commissioner of Education, Fiscal Year 1975* (Washington, DC: Government Printing Office, 1976), table 17.

from around 2 percent in 1945 to around 8 percent in the early 1970s. Under the shadow of the Cold War, congressional appropriations for research, expansion of higher education, and the GI Bill powered what Patricia Gumport and her associates dubbed "the massification of higher education."[28] Importantly, expansion in the number and carrying capacity of two- and four-year postsecondary institutions permitted unprecedented college access to historically underrepresented ethnic and income groups. The coincidence of the oversized baby boom cohorts with the massification of higher education not only increased the national stock of human capital but also raised productivity and stimulated innovation.[29]

Large numbers of college-educated workers enabled the United States to realize a productivity boost via higher savings and capital investments. But demographic dividends are not automatic; they require sustained investment in high-quality education so that subsequent youth cohorts also can maximize their productivity when they join the labor force. To the detriment of the nation, the commitment to education waned in the aftermath of the 1973 oil crisis, the failed Vietnam War, and the sharp budget cuts prompted by the stagflation of the early 1980s. Federal expenditures on education remained below 5 percent of GDP from 1986 to 1999, and have fluctuated between 5.1 and 5.5 percent since 2001.[30] Consequently, gains in educational attainment have slowed since 1990 and hindered the rate of technological innovation and economic growth.[31] Following the Great Recession, the nation's commitment to education as a national priority has once again waned, as noted earlier, but with worrisome implications for social fragmentation when mapped against the backdrop of demographic diversification coupled with population aging.

Although the United States was once a leader in the share of its population with college degrees, the nation's underinvestment in higher education is evident in the slowing cohort gains in bachelor's degree attainment rates. To appreciate how far the United States has slipped in college attainment, it is instructive to compare the BA completion rates of 55- to 64-year-olds with 25- to 34-year-olds (the current cohort of the age when most higher education is completed), shown in table 7.1. It bears emphasizing that seniors ages 55–64 in 2010 not only are members of the baby boom generation, which posed a huge strain on educational systems, but also were beneficiaries of the massification of higher education. The cohort shares attaining bachelor's degrees more than doubled for seniors born between 1950 and 1980; changes in the share of BA recipients among 25- to 34-year-olds were much flatter, however. Slightly less than

TABLE 7.1. Changes in Cohort BA Attainment Rates,
1980–2010 (percentages)

Age cohort	1980	1990	2000	2010
25–34 yrs.	23.3	22.8	27.6	31.2
55–64 yrs.	11.6	16.8	22.5	28.4
Difference	11.7	6.0	5.1	2.8

Sources: U.S Census Bureau, *Decennial Census of Population*, 1980–2000, and *American Community Survey*, 2010

one in four adults ages 25–34 in 1980 had completed a baccalaureate degree; by 2010, the comparable share had risen only eight percentage points. Evidence of intercohort progress requires rising or at least stable gaps, but the bottom row shows an intercohort slowdown in BA attainment rates.

One might argue that the United States has reached a threshold beyond which further gains are unlikely, but a comparison of trends in other OECD nations suggests that the United States has been losing its competitive edge relative to some of its peers.[32] In 2010, the United States ranked behind Korea, Canada, Russia, and Norway in the percentages of 25- to 34-year-olds completing four-year college degrees. The United States ranks fourth out of thirty-six OECD nations for the older cohort and twelfth for the younger cohort.[33] Figure 7.2 reveals the significance for social integration of the nation's slowdown in BA attainment rates among 25- to 34-year-olds, whose labor market activity is fundamental for the well-being of the aging baby boom generations. The good news is that BA attainment rates rose for all groups; the bad news is that the attainment gaps between blacks and Hispanics, on the one hand, and whites, on the other, widened. Specifically, the black-white attainment gap rose from 14.5 percent to 18.8 percent between 1980 and 2011; for Hispanics, the BA attainment gap rose from 18 to 26 percent, an increase of

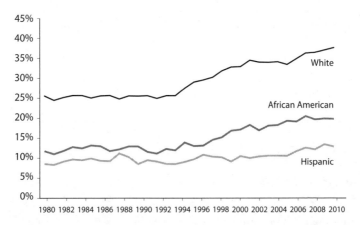

FIGURE 7.2. BA Attainment Rates for 25- to 34-Year-Olds, 1980–2011
Source: Demos and Young Invincibles, *The State of Young America* (Demos, 2011).

8 percentage points. This trend is worrisome because Hispanics are the fastest-growing youth population in the United States and, as such, their social and economic fortunes will be pivotal for the future of the nation. What kind of future that will be is highly uncertain.[34]

The United States has been losing ground to its competitors on other fronts as well. Following the Soviet Union's successful launch of Sputnik in 1957, the federal government created the National Science Foundation and consolidated support for research and development (R&D); in response to growing competition and technological innovation from Asia, it further bolstered investments in R&D.[35] These investments have faltered in recent years. Figure 7.3 shows that U.S. R&D spending has been relatively flat since 1992 and that Germany, Israel, Japan, and South Korea invest larger shares of their GDP in R&D. China, currently the second-largest economy, has been increasing its R&D

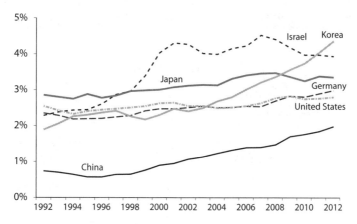

FIGURE 7.3. R&D Expenditures as a Percentage of GDP, 1992–2012: Selected OECD Nations and China
Source: http://stats.oecd.org/Index.aspx?DataSetCode=MSTI_PUB#

spending since 2000. The United States still outspends China in R&D, but the gap has been closing. Furthermore, China has been making massive investments in higher education, determined to outcompete the United States as it transitions to a global power.

The legacy of higher education expansion as the baby boom cohorts came of age is clearly evident in the age-education pyramid shown in figure 7.4. In the interest of parsimony and to highlight important contrasts in the destinies of America's dependents, I pooled all racial and ethnic groups in the right pyramid.[36] The diversification of the school-age population is clearly evident in the large youth cohorts on the right base of the pyramid compared with the shrinking white cohorts on the left base. The beneficiaries of higher education massification coincide with the large boomer cohorts and their descendants, but relatively smaller gains obtained for U.S. minority groups. A comparable

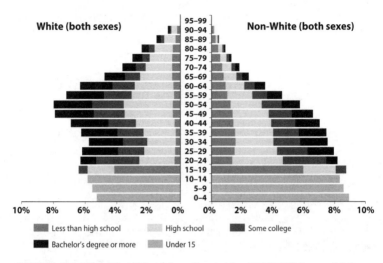

FIGURE 7.4. U.S. Age-Education Pyramids, 2010: White and Non-white Populations

Source: U.S. Census Bureau, *American Community Survey*, 2010, one-year estimate

pyramid comparing Hispanics and whites would dramatize the diverging destinies of America's dependents even more because Hispanics have the highest fertility rates and also the lowest educational attainment rates.

The Path Forward

The 2014 school year was an important milestone in the diversity of American education: for the first time in history, the majority of elementary and secondary school students were black, Hispanic, Asian, or Native American.[37] Diversification is not a transitory feature of the U.S. population, but the implications for social cohesion are highly uncertain. The changing demography of the school-age population provides an opportunity to reap a demographic dividend as minority fertility drops; however, in light of rising inequality, stagnant social mobility, and the retirement of the baby boom cohorts, the generational transition also represents a formidable risk for the nation.

As the richest country in the world, the United States has the resources to capitalize on diversity by revitalizing its social contract with youth. That minority youths are coming of age in an aging white society is a compelling reason for the nation to ramp up human capital investments, to close achievement gaps, and raise college attainment rates in order to ensure that the burgeoning minority youth cohorts are equipped to meet the support demands of the aging population. U.S. economic history shows that increases in the stock of human capital, and college-educated workers in particular, can galvanize the economy, spur social mobility, and restore broadly shared prosperity. Expanding the nation's human capital stock to ensure sustained growth requires a steadfast commitment to educational investments—even during economic downturns. My concern is that the nation lacks a unifying motive comparable to that witnessed during the Cold War that will keep our compelling interests in sharp focus. Political will, not population growth and diversification, remains the ultimate challenge.

Notes

Introduction

1. Lovanie Pomplilus, in *Social Justice Learning Community* (Rutgers University–Newark, 2015), PDF file.
2. Ibid.
3. Christian Quiroz, in ibid.
4. Lani Guinier, *The Tyranny of the Meritocracy: Democratizing Higher Education in America* (Boston: Beacon Press, 2015). See also http://www.oecd.org/edu/Education-at-a-Glance-2014.pdf.
5. Frank Bruni, "Demanding More from College," *New York Times*, September 6, 2014.
6. Raj Chetty, Nathaniel Hendren, Patrick Kline, Emmanuel Saez, and Nicholas Turner, "Is the United States Still a Land of Opportunity? Recent Trends in Intergenerational Mobility" (NBER Working Paper Series, National Bureau of Economic Research, January 2014) (http://www.equality-of-opportunity.org/images/mobility_trends.pdf).
7. Gary Orfield and John Yun, "Resegregation in American Schools" (The Civil Rights Project, UCLA, January 1, 1999); Paul A. Jargowsky, "Architecture of Segregation: Civil Unrest, the Concentration of Poverty, and Public Policy" (Century Foundation Issue Brief, August 9, 2015); Editorial, "The Architecture of Segregation," *New York Times*, September 6, 2015, p. SR8; Douglas S. Massey and Nancy A. Denton, *American Apartheid: Segregation and the Making of the Underclass* (Cambridge, MA: Harvard University Press, 1993).
8. Michelle Alexander, *The New Jim Crow: Mass Incarceration in the Age of Colorblindness* (New York: New Press, 2010).
9. Chief Justice John Roberts opinion, Parents Involved in Community Schools v. Seattle School District No. 1, 551 U.S. at 748 (2007).

10. Marta Tienda, "Diversity Is Not Equal to Inclusion: Translating Access into Equity in Higher Education," *Education Researcher* 42 (2013): 467–475; Rupert W. Nacoste, *Taking on Diversity: How We Can Move from Anxiety to Respect* (Amherst, NY: Prometheus Books, 2015); Patricia Gurin, Biren Nagda, and Ximena Zúñiga, *Dialogue across Difference: Practice, Theory, and Research on Intergroup Dialogue* (New York: Russell Sage Foundation, 2013).
11. Charles Tilly, *Durable Inequality* (Berkeley and Los Angeles: University of California Press, 1998).
12. Editorial, "The Architecture of Segregation"; Nancy Cantor, "Mirror, Mirror: Reflections on Race and the Visage of Higher Education in America," *The Conversation*, June 23, 2015.
13. Patricia Gurin, Jeffrey Lehman, and Earl Lewis, *Defending Diversity: Affirmative Action at the University of Michigan* (Ann Arbor: University of Michigan Press, 2004).
14. Lawrence Bobo, personal communication, December 2014.

The "Diversity Explosion" Is America's Twenty-first-Century Baby Boom

1. This essay is adapted, with permission, from William H. Frey, *Diversity Explosion: How New Racial Demographics Are Remaking America* (Washington, DC: Brookings Institution Press, 2015), chapters 1 and 12.
2. Sabrina Tavernise, "Whites Account for Under Half of Births in U.S.," *New York Times*, May 17, 2012, p. A1 (http://www.nytimes.com/2012/05/17/us/whites-account-for-under-half-of-births-in-us.html?_r=0).
3. Frey, *Diversity Explosion*, chapter 6, "The Great Migration of Blacks: In Reverse."
4. The white 18- to 29-year-old population is now experiencing a decline and the white 30- to 44-year-old population is projected to decline after the year 2034. Author's calculations of U.S. Census Bureau Projection data released December 2012 (http://www.census.gov/population/projections/data/national/2012.html).
5. William H. Frey, "Immigrant and Native Migrant Magnets," *American Demographics*, November 1996, pp. 1–5; William H. Frey and Jonathan Tilove, "Immigrants In, Native Whites Out," *New York Times Magazine*, August 20, 1995, pp. 44–45; William H. Frey and Kao-Lee Liaw, "The Impact of Recent Immigration on Population Redistribution within the United States," in *The Immigration Debate: Studies of Economic, Demographic and Fiscal Effects of*

Immigration, ed. James P. Smith and Barry Edmonston (Washington, DC: National Academy Press, 1998), pp. 388–448.

6. William H. Frey, "Diversity Spreads Out: Metropolitan Shifts in Hispanic, Asian, and Black Populations since 2000," Living Cities Census Series (Metropolitan Policy Program, Brookings Institution, March 2006), pp. 1–26 (http://www.frey-demographer.org /reports/R-2006-1_DiversitySpreadsOut.pdf); William H. Frey and Kao-Lee Liaw, "Interstate Migration of Hispanics, Asians, and Blacks: Cultural Constraints and Middle-Class Flight" (report prepared for the University of Michigan Population Studies Center, May 2005) (http://www.psc.isr.umich.edu/pubs/pdf/rr05-575.pdf).

7. Frey, *Diversity Explosion*, chapter 8, "Melting Pot Cities and Suburbs."

8. Frey, *Diversity Explosion*, chapter 9, "Neighborhood Segregation toward a New Racial Paradigm."

9. Frey, *Diversity Explosion*, chapter 10, "Multiracial Marriages and Multiracial America."

10. Frey, *Diversity Explosion*, chapter 11, "Race and Politics: Expanding the Battleground."

11. Frey, *Diversity Explosion*, pp. 66–70, 87–94, 108–114.

12. U.S. Bureau of Labor Statistics, "Labor Force Characteristics by Race and Ethnicity, 2012," BLS Reports (Department of Labor, 2013) (http://www.bls.gov/cps/cpsrace2011.pdf); Christian E. Weller and Farah Ahmad, "The State of Communities of Color in the U.S. Economy" (Washington, DC: Center for American Progress, 2013) (http:// www.americanprogress.org/wp-content/uploads/2013/10/Commu nitiesOfColor-4.pdf); Pew Research Center, "Wealth Gaps Rise to Record Highs between Whites, Blacks, and Hispanics" (Pew Research Center, 2011) (http://www.pewsocialtrends.org/files/2011/07 /SDT-Wealth-Report_7-26-11_FINAL.pdf).

13. Jeffrey S. Passel, "Demography of Immigrant Youth: Past, Present and Future," *Future of Children* 21, no. 1 (Spring 2011): 19–41 (http://futureofchildren.org/futureofchildren/publications/docs /21_01_02.pdf); Richard Fry and Jeffrey S. Passell, "Latino Children: A Majority Are U.S.-Born Offspring of Immigrants" (Pew Research Center, May 2009) (http://pewhispanic.org/files/reports/110 .pdf).

14. Richard Fry and Paul Taylor, "Hispanic High School Graduates Pass Whites in Rate of College Enrollment" (Pew Research Center, May 2013) (http://www.pewhispanic.org/files/2013/05/PHC_college _enrollment_2013-05.pdf); Dowell Myers and John Pitkin, "Assimilation Today: New Evidence Shows the Latest Immigrants to

America Are Following in Our History's Footsteps" (Center for American Progress, September 2010) (www.americanprogress.org /issues/2010/09/pdf/immigrant_assimilation.pdf); Julie Park and Dowell Myers, "Intergenerational Mobility in the Post-1965 Immigration Era: Estimates by an Immigrant Generation Cohort Method," *Demography* 47, no. 2 (May 2010): 369–392.

15. Gary Orfield, John Kucsera, and Genevieve Siegel-Hawley, "*E Pluribus* . . . Separation: Deepening Double Segregation for More Students" (UCLA Civil Rights Project/Proyecto Derechos Civiles, September 2012) (http://civilrightsproject.ucla.edu/research/k-12 -education/integration-and-diversity/mlk-national/e-pluribus . . . separation-deepening-double-segregation-for-more-students/orfield _epluribus_revised_omplete_2012.pdf).

16. Ibid.

17. Anthony P. Carnevale and Nicole Smith, "America's Future Workforce," in *All-In Nation: An America That Works for All*, ed. Vanessa Cardenas and Sarah Treuhaft (Washington, DC: Center for America Progress and PolicyLink, 2013), pp. 32–45 (http://www.all innation.org/pdf/AllInNation.pdf).

18. An overview of barriers is provided in Daniel T. Lichter, "Integration or Fragmentation? Racial Diversity and the American Future," *Demography* 50 (2013): 359–391.

19. One study classified state immigration legislation over several years through 2008 on a scale from "integrative" to "punitive." Seven of the eight Melting Pot states were classified as "integrative" or "somewhat integrative," whereas all of the fourteen states classified as "punitive" or "somewhat punitive" were located in New Sun Belt or Heartland states. See Progressive States Network, "The Anti-Immigrant Movement That Failed" (September 2008) (http://www .progressivestates.org/files/reports/immigrationSept08.pdf). A 2007 analysis of local housing ordinances that target immigrants found that ordinances were correlated not with the size of a locality's foreign-born or Hispanic population but rather with a rapid increase in the foreign-born or Hispanic share of the population since 2000. See Jill Esbenshade, "Division and Dislocation: Regulating Immigration through Local Housing Ordinances" (Immigration Policy Center, Summer 2007) (http://www.immigrationpolicy.org/sites/default /files/docs/IPC%20Special%20Report%20PR.pdf). Another analysis of local municipalities emphasizes the pace of immigrant population growth as a predictor of exclusionary policies. See Kyle E. Walker and Helga Leitner, "The Variegated Landscape of Local Immigration Policies in the United States," *Urban Geography* 32 (2011):

156–178 (http://www.sscnet.ucla.edu/geog/downloads/7235/494
.pdf).

20. Ricardo Gambetta and Zivile Gedrimalte, "Municipal Innovations
in Immigrant Integration: 20 Cities, 20 Good Practices." American
Cities Series (National League of Cities, 2010) (http://www.nlc.org
/Documents/Find%20City%20Solutions/Research%20Innovation
/Immigrant%20Integration/municipal-innovations-immigrant-
integration-20-cities-sep10.pdf); Hall et al., "The Geography of Immigrant Skills: Educational Profiles of Metropolitan Areas" (Brookings Metropolitan Policy Program, 2011), pp. 20–21 (http://www
.brookings.edu/~/media/research/files/papers/2011/6/immi
grants%20singer/06_immigrants_singer.pdf).

21. Frey, *Diversity Explosion*, chapter 11, "Race and Politics: Expanding the Battleground."

22. This is demonstrated in a study that shows support for school financing to be negatively related to the portion of elderly individuals who age in place within the community, a relationship that is
heightened when the school-age population is heavily nonwhite. See
David N. Figlio and Deborah Fletcher, "Suburbanization, Demographic Change, and the Consequences for School Finance," *Journal of Public Economics*, no. 96 (2012): 1144–1153.

23. Ronald Brownstein, "The Gray and the Brown: The Generational
Mismatch," *National Journal*, July 24, 2010, pp. 14–22 (http://www
.nationaljournal.com/magazine/the-gray-and-the-brown-the
-generational-mismatch-20100724).

24. A similar case is made about the relationship between immigrants
and the baby boom generation in Dowell Myers, *Immigrants and
Boomers: Forging a New Social Contract for the Future of America*
(New York: Russell Sage Foundation, 2007).

25. See Generations United, "Out of Many, One: Uniting the Changing
Faces of America" (Generations United and Generations Initiative,
2013) (http://www.gu.org/LinkClick.aspx?fileticket=_Te_mh9O
znI%3d&tabid=475&mid=1049); and Cardenas and Treuhaft,
All-In Nation (http://images2.americanprogress.org/CAP/2013/12
/AllInNation.pdf).

26. Mitra Toosi, "Labor Force Projections to 2020: A More Slowly
Growing Workforce," *Monthly Labor Review*, January 2012, pp.
43–63 (http://www.bls.gov/opub/mlr/2012/01/art3full.pdf); Anthony P. Carnavale, Nicole Smith, and Jeff Strohl, "Help Wanted:
Projections of Jobs and Education Requirements through 2018"
(Georgetown University Center on Education and the Workforce,
2010) (http://www9.georgetown.edu/grad/gppi/hpi/cew/pdfs/full

report.pdf); Dowell Myers, Stephen Levy, and John Pitkin, "The Contributions of Immigrants and Their Children to the American Workforce and Jobs of the Future" (Center for American Progress, June 2013) (http://www.americanprogress.org/wp-content/uploads /2013/06/OurFutureTogether.pdf).

27. Richard Alba, *Blurring the Color Line: The New Chance for a More Integrated America* (Cambridge, MA: Harvard University Press, 2009).

28. This point is made in Richard Alba and Victor Nee, *Remaking the American Mainstream: Assimilation and Contemporary Immigration* (Cambridge, MA: Harvard University Press, 2003), chapter 7.

Chapter 1: Less Separate, Still Unequal

1. My thanks to K. Anthony Appiah, Patricia Gurin, Ira Katznelson, and Marta Tienda for detailed comments.

2. Marta Tienda, "Diversity ≠ Inclusion: Translating Access into Equity in Higher Education," *Education Researcher* 42 (2013): 467–475.

3. Charles Tilly, *Durable Inequality* (Berkeley and Los Angeles: University of California Press, 1998).

4. Glenn Loury, *The Anatomy of Racial Inequality* (Cambridge, MA: Harvard University Press, 2002); Daria Roithmayr, *Reproducing Racism: How Everyday Choices Lock in White Advantage* (New York: New York University Press, 2014).

5. President Lyndon B. Johnson's Remarks at the Signing of the Immigration Bill, Liberty Island, New York, October 3, 1965, Lyndon Baines Johnson Presidential Library, Austin, Texas (http://www.lbjlib .utexas.edu/johnson/archives.hom/speeches.hom/651003.asp).

6. Most scholars and the public use the terms *Hispanic* and *Latino* interchangeably. The U.S. Census Bureau began using the term *Hispanic* in the mid-1970s. For the sake of consistency, I use the term *Hispanic*. A recent Pew Research Center Hispanic Trends Survey shows that 50 percent of Hispanic/Latino respondents do not have strong preferences for either term; 33 percent prefer *Hispanic*, and 15 percent prefer *Latino*. See Mark Hugo Lopez, "Hispanic or Latino: Many Don't Care Except in Texas" (Pew Research Center, October 28, 2013) (http://www.pewresearch.org/fact-tank/2013/10/28 /in-texas-its-hispanic-por-favor/).

7. Sharon R. Ennis, Merarys Ríos-Vargas, and Nora G. Albert, *The Hispanic Population 2010*, 2010 Census Briefs (Washington, DC: U.S. Bureau of the Census, 2011).

8. An indispensable overview of Hispanic residential patterns can be found in Marta Tienda and Norma Fuentes, "Hispanics in Metropolitan America: New Realities and Old Debates," *Annual Review of Sociology* 40 (2014): 499–520.

9. Barrett A. Lee, John Iceland, and Gregory Sharp, "Racial and Ethnic Diversity Goes Local: Charting Change in American Communities over Three Decades" (Russell Sage Foundation and Brown University, US2010 Project, September 2012) (http://www.s4.brown.edu /us2010/Data/Report/report08292012.pdf).

10. Michael Jones-Correa, "Reshaping the American Dream: Immigrants, Ethnic Minorities, and the Politics of the New Suburbs," in *The New Suburban History*, ed. Kevin M. Kruse and Thomas J. Sugrue (Chicago: University of Chicago Press, 2006), pp. 183–204; Audrey Singer, "The Rise of the New Immigrant Gateways" (Brookings Institution, Living Cities Census Series, February 2004) (http://www .brookings.edu/urban/pubs/20040301_gateways.pdf); Kimberley S. Johnson, "Black Suburbanization: American Dream or the New Banlieue?" (Social Science Research Council, Cities Papers, 2014) (http:// citiespapers.ssrc.org/black-suburbanization-american-dream-or-the -new-banlieue/). On postwar suburbs, see Kenneth T. Jackson, *Crabgrass Frontier: The Suburbanization of the United States* (New York: Oxford University Press, 1985); Andrew Wiese, *Places of Their Own: African American Suburbanization in the Twentieth Century* (Chicago: University of Chicago Press, 2004); Thomas J. Sugrue, "Suburbanization and African Americans," in *Encarta Africana*, ed. K. Anthony Appiah and Henry Louis Gates, third edition, CD-ROM (Cambridge and Seattle: Microsoft/Afropaedia LLC, 1999); William H. Frey, "Melting Pot Cities and Suburbs: Racial and Ethnic Change in Metro America in the 2000s" (State of Metropolitan America, Metropolitan Policy Program, Brookings Institution, May 2011) (http://www.brookings.edu/~/media/research/files/papers/2011 /5/04%20census%20ethnicity%20frey/0504_census_ethnicity_frey .pdf).

11. For a useful summary, see Margery Austin Turner and Stephen L. Ross, "How Racial Discrimination Affects the Search for Housing," in *The Geography of Opportunity: Race and Housing Choice in Metropolitan America*, ed. Xavier de Souza Briggs (Washington, DC: Brookings Institution Press, 2005), pp. 81–100. For detailed reports, see Margery Austin Turner et al., *Discrimination in Metropolitan Housing Markets: National Results from Phase 1 HDS 2000* (Washington, DC: Urban Institute and U.S. Department of Housing and Urban Development, 2002) (http://www.huduser.org

/Publications/pdf/Phase1_Report.pdf). Earlier studies of steering and discrimination include Diana Pearce, "Gatekeepers and Homeseekers: Institutionalized Patterns in Racial Steering," *Social Problems* 26 (1979): 325–342; Douglas S. Massey and Nancy A. Denton, *American Apartheid: Segregation and the Making of the Underclass* (Cambridge, MA: Harvard University Press, 1993), pp. 98–104; John Yinger, *Housing Discrimination Study: Incidence of Discrimination and Variation in Discriminatory Behavior* (Washington, DC: U.S. Department of Housing and Urban Development, 1991); John Yinger, *Closed Doors, Opportunities Lost: The Continuing Costs of Housing Discrimination* (New York: Russell Sage Foundation, 1995); Michael Fix and Raymond J. Struyk, eds., *Clear and Convincing Evidence: Measurement of Discrimination in America* (Washington, DC: Urban Institute Press, 1993).

12. Douglas S. Massey and Garvey Lundy, "Use of Black English and Racial Discrimination in Urban Housing Markets," *Urban Affairs Review* 36 (2001): 452–469.

13. Massey and Denton, *American Apartheid*; Jacob Rugh and Douglas S. Massey, "Segregation in Post–Civil Rights America: Stalled Integration or End of the Segregated Century?" *Du Bois Review* 11, no. 2 (2014): 205–232.

14. Rugh and Massey, "Segregation in Post–Civil Rights America." For 2000 data, see Xavier de Sousa Briggs, "More *Pluribus*, Less *Unum*? The Changing Geography of Race and Opportunity," in Briggs, *The Geography of Opportunity*, pp. 24–25.

15. Charles Moskos and John Sibley Butler, *All That We Can Be: Black Leadership and Racial Integration the Army Way* (New York: Basic Books, 1996); Cardell K. Jacobson and Tim B. Heaton, "Intergroup Marriage and United States Military Service," *Journal of Political and Military Service* 31 (2003): 1–22. Rugh and Massey, "Segregation in Post–Civil Rights America," find that each point increase in the log of the military population per 100,000 persons reduces racial-ethnic dissimilarity by 0.503 points. On the military generally, see also Brief for Lt. General Julius W. Becton Jr. et al. as Amici Curiae Supporting Respondents, Grutter v. Bollinger, et al., 539 U.S. 306 (2003) (http://www.vpcomm.umich.edu/admissions/legal/gru_amicus-ussc/um/MilitaryL-both.pdf).

16. It is important to recall that diversity in higher education is a first step toward inclusion and equality, and to be successful requires other measures to foster contact and interaction. On this point, see Tienda, "Diversity ≠ Inclusion."

17. Mary J. Fischer and Marta Tienda, "Redrawing Spatial Color Lines: Hispanic Metropolitan Dispersal, Segregation, and Economic Opportunity," in *Hispanics and the Future of America*, ed. Marta Tienda and Faith Mitchell (Washington, DC: National Academies Press, 2006), quotation on p. 102.
18. On the segregation of Afro-Hispanics see, among others, Douglas S. Massey, "Hispanic Residential Segregation: A Comparison of Mexicans, Cubans, and Puerto Ricans," *Sociology and Social Research* 65 (1981): 311–322; and John Iceland and Kyle Anne Nelson, "Hispanic Segregation in Metropolitan America: Exploring the Multiple Forms of Spatial Assimilation," *American Sociological Review* 73 (2008): 741–765.
19. Eric Fong and Kumiko Shibuya, "Multiethnic Cities in North America," *Annual Review of Sociology* 31 (2005): 285–304; Rugh and Massey, "Segregation in Post–Civil Rights America"; Daniel T. Lichter, Domenico Parisi, Michael C. Taquino, and Steven Michael Grice, "Residential Segregation in New Hispanic Destinations: Cities, Suburbs, and Rural Communities Compared," *Social Science Review* 39 (2010): 215–230.
20. Lawrence D. Bobo, Melvin L. Oliver, James H. Johnson Jr., and Abel Valenzuela Jr., *Prismatic Metropolis: Inequality in Los Angeles* (New York: Russell Sage Foundation, 1999); Camille Zubrinsky Charles, *Won't You Be My Neighbor? Race, Class, and Residence in Los Angeles* (New York: Russell Sage Foundation, 2006).
21. William Julius Wilson and Richard Taub, *There Goes the Neighborhood: Racial, Ethnic, and Class Tensions in Four Chicago Neighborhoods and Their Meaning for America* (New York: Knopf, 2006).
22. John Iceland and Cynthia Lake, "Immigrant Residential Patterns in U.S. Metropolitan Areas, 1990–2000" (paper presented to the 2005 Population Association of America conference) (http://paa2005.princeton.edu/papers/50615).
23. Reynolds Farley, "Racial Identities in 2000," in *The New Race Question*, ed. Joel Perlmann and Mary C. Waters (New York: Russell Sage Foundation, 2002); Sonya M. Tafoya, Hans Johnson, and Laura E. Hill, "Who Chooses to Choose Two?" in *The American People: Census 2000*, ed. Reynolds Farley and John Haaga (New York: Russell Sage Foundation, 2005), pp. 332–351; Jennifer Lee and Frank D. Bean, "Reinventing the Color Line: Immigration and America's New Racial/Ethnic Divide," *Social Forces* 86 (2007): 561–586.
24. Tienda and Fuentes, "Hispanics in Metropolitan America."

25. John R. Logan, Deirdre Oakley, and Jacob Stowell, "School Segregation in Metropolitan Regions, 1970–2000: The Impacts of Policy Choices on Public Education," *American Journal of Sociology* 113, no. 6 (May 2008): 1611–1644.
26. Christine H. Rossell and David Armor, "The Effectiveness of School Desegregation Plans, 1968–1991," *American Politics Quarterly* 24 (1996): 267–302.
27. Davison M. Douglas, *Reading, Writing, and Race: The Desegregation of the Charlotte Schools* (Chapel Hill: University of North Carolina Press, 1995); Matthew Lassiter, "'Socioeconomic Integration' in the Suburbs: From Reactionary Populism to Class Fairness in Metropolitan Charlotte," in *The New Suburban History*, ed. Kruse and Sugrue.
28. Milliken v. Bradley, 418 U.S. 717 (1974); Paul Dimond, *Beyond Busing: Inside the Challenge to Urban Segregation* (Ann Arbor: University of Michigan Press, 1985); Thomas J. Sugrue, *Sweet Land of Liberty: The Forgotten Struggle for Civil Rights in the North* (New York: Random House, 2008), chapter 13.
29. Gary Orfield, *Schools More Separate: Consequences of a Decade of Resegregation* (Cambridge, MA: Harvard University Civil Rights Project, 2001).
30. Sean F. Reardon and John T. Yun, "Integrating Neighborhoods, Segregating Schools: The Retreat from School Desegregation in the South, 1990–2000," *North Carolina Law Review* 81 (2003): 1563–1596; Capacchione v. Charlotte-Mecklenburg Schools, 57 F. Supp. 2d 228 (1999); Parents Involved in Community Schools v. Seattle School District No. 1, 551 U.S. 701 (2007).
31. Reardon and Yun, "Integrating Neighborhoods, Segregating Schools"; Capacchione v. Charlotte-Mecklenburg Schools; Parents Involved.
32. Allen Finder, "As Test Scores Jump, Raleigh Credits Integration by Income," *New York Times*, September 25, 2005; Michael Winerip, "Seeking Integration, Whatever the Path," *New York Times*, February 27, 2011.
33. Gary Orfield, John Kucsera, and Genevieve Siegel-Hawley, "*E Pluribus* . . . Separation: Deepening Double Segregation for More Students" (UCLA Civil Rights Project/Proyecto Derechos Civiles, September 2012), p. 9; Paul Jargowsky and Mohamed El Komi, "Before or After the Bell? School Context and Neighborhood Effects on Student Achievement," in *Neighborhood and Life Chances: How Place Matters in Modern America*, ed. Harriet B. Newburger,

Eugenie I., Birch, and Susan M. Wachter (Philadelphia: University of Pennsylvania Press, 2011), pp. 50–72.

34. Gary Orfield and Chungmei Lee, *Why Segregation Matters: Poverty and Educational Inequality* (Cambridge, MA: Civil Rights Project, Harvard University, 2005) (http://escholarship.org/uc/item/4xr 8z4wb).

35. U.S. Department of Education, Office for Civil Rights, *Civil Rights Data Collection, Data Snapshot: School Discipline, Issue Brief, No. 1* (March 2014) (http://www2.ed.gov/about/offices/list/ocr/docs /crdc-discipline-snapshot.pdf); Russell Skiba et al., "The Color of Discipline: Sources of Racial and Gender Disproportionality in School Punishment," *Urban Review* 34 (2002): 317–342; Jacob Kang-Brown, Jennifer Trone, Jennifer Fratello, and Tarika Daftary-Kapur, "A Generation Later: What We Have Learned about Zero Tolerance Programs" (Issue Brief, Vera Institute for Justice, December 2013) (http://www.vera.org/sites/default/files/resources/downloads /zero-tolerance-in-schools-policy-brief.pdf).

36. Orfield, Kucsera, and Siegel-Hawley, "*E Pluribus . . .* Separation."

37. Tom Romero II, "A Raza Latino? Multiracial Ambivalence, Color Denial, and the Emergence of a Tri-Ethnic Jurisprudence at the End of the Twentieth Century," *New Mexico Law Review* 37, no. 2 (2007): 245–306.

38. Sean F. Reardon and John T. Yun, "Suburban Racial Change and Suburban School Segregation, 1987–95," *Sociology of Education* 74 (2001): 79–101; Fischer and Tienda, "Redrawing Spatial Color Lines," p. 121.

39. Marcelo M. Suárez-Orozco and Mariela Páez, eds., *Latinos: Remaking America* (Berkeley and Los Angeles: University of California Press, 2009), p. 8.

40. Edmund Hamann, Stanton Wortham, and Enrique G. Murillo Jr., "Education and Policy in the New Latino Diaspora," in *Education in the New Latino Diaspora: Policy and the Politics of Identity*, ed. Stanton Wortham, Enrique G. Murillo Jr., and Edmund T. Hamann (Westport, CT: Ablex Publishing, 2002). See also Luis C. Moll and Richard Ruiz, "The Schooling of Latino Children," in *Latinos: Remaking America*, ed. Suárez-Orozco and Páez, pp. 362–374.

41. U.S. Department of Education, Institute of Education Sciences, National Center for Education Statistics, *Digest of Education Statistics*, 2013, table 219.70 (http://nces.ed.gov/programs/digest/d13/tables /dt13_219.70.asp). These data do not include place of birth. But other studies suggest that foreign-born Hispanics are far more likely

to drop out of school than the native born. For this point, see Marta Tienda, *Hispanicity and Educational Inequality: Risks, Opportunities and the Nation's Future*, Tomas Rivera Lecture, Educational Testing Service (Princeton, NJ: ETS, 2009).

42. Patricia C. Gándara and Frances Contreras, *The Latino Education Crisis: The Consequence of Failed Social Policies* (Cambridge, MA: Harvard University Press, 2009), chapter 6.

43. For historical unemployment data, see Robert W. Fairlie and William A. Sundstrom, "The Emergence, Persistence, and Recent Widening of the Racial Employment Gap," *Industrial and Labor Relations Review* 52 (1999): 252–270. Their employment statistics are seasonally adjusted and include the nonschool, noninstitutionalized male population ages 16–64. For an update, see Pew Research Center, "Black Unemployment Rate Consistently Twice That of Whites" (August 21, 2013) (http://www.pewresearch.org/fact-tank/2013/08/21/through-good-times-and-bad-black-unemployment-is-consistently-double-that-of-whites/). Pew draws from Bureau of Labor Statistics reports from 1954 to 2012.

44. Joleen Kirschenman and Kathryn Neckerman, "We'd Love to Hire Them, But . . . The Meaning of Race for Employers," in *The Urban Underclass*, ed. Christopher Jencks and Paul E. Peterson (Washington, DC: Brookings Institution, 1991), pp. 203–232; William Julius Wilson, *When Work Disappears: The World of the New Urban Poor* (New York: Knopf, 1996); Philip Moss and Chris Tilly, *Stories Employers Tell: Race, Skill, and Hiring in America* (New York: Russell Sage Foundation, 2001).

45. Kirschenman and Neckerman, "We'd Love to Hire Them"; Marianne Bertrand and Sendhil Mullainathan, "Are Emily and Greg More Employable Than Lakisha and Jamal? A Field Experiment on Labor Market Discrimination," *American Economic Review* 94 (2004): 991–1013; Chris Tilly et al., "Space as a Signal: How Employers Perceive Neighborhoods in Four Metropolitan Labor Markets," in *Urban Inequality: Evidence from Four Cities*, ed. Alice O'Connor, Chris Tilly, and Lawrence Bobo (New York: Russell Sage Foundation, 2001), pp. 304–339; Keith R. Ihlanfeldt and David L. Sjoquist, "The Spatial Mismatch Hypothesis: A Review of Recent Studies and Their Implications for Welfare Reform," *Housing Policy Debate* 9 (1998): 849–892; Devah Pager, "The Use of Field Experiments for Studies of Employment Discrimination: Contributions, Critiques, and Directions for the Future," *Annals of the American Academy of Political and Social Science* 609 (2007): 104–133.

46. For an overview, see Heather Ann Thompson, "Why Mass Incarceration Matters: Rethinking Crisis, Decline, and Transformation in Postwar American History," *Journal of American History* 97 (2010): 703–734.

47. U.S. Department of Justice, Office of Justice Programs, Bureau of Justice Statistics, "Correctional Populations in the United States, 2010," NCJ 236319, *BJS Bulletin*, December 2011.

48. Devah Pager, *Marked: Race, Crime, and Finding Work in an Age of Mass Incarceration* (Chicago: University of Chicago Press, 2007). See also Harry J. Holzer, Paul Offner, and Elaine Sorensen, "Declining Employment of Young, Black, Less-Educated Men: The Role of Incarceration and Child Support," *Journal of Policy Analysis and Management* 24 (2005): 329–350.

49. U.S. Census Bureau, Current Population Reports, P60-249, *Income and Poverty in the United States: 2013* (Washington, DC: U.S. Government Printing Office, 2014). Hereafter referred to as U.S. Census, *Income and Poverty 2013*. Data compiled from U.S. Census Bureau, *Current Population Survey*, 1960 to 2014, Annual Social and Economic Supplements.

50. Patrick Sharkey, *Stuck in Place: Urban Neighborhoods and the End of Progress Toward Racial Equality* (Chicago: University of Chicago Press, 2013), pp. 2–3.

51. U.S. Census, *Income and Poverty 2013*.

52. Ibid.

53. Cordelia Reimers, "Economic Well-Being," in *Hispanics and the Future of America*, ed. Tienda, pp. 291–361.

54. U.S. Census, *Income and Poverty 2013*.

55. All of the quotes in this paragraph come from Melvin L. Oliver and Thomas M. Shapiro, *Black Wealth, White Wealth: A New Perspective on Racial Inequality* (New York: Routledge, 1997), pp. 5–6.

56. U.S. Census Bureau, "Residential Vacancies and Homeownership in the Third Quarter 2014," *U.S. Census Bureau News*, October 28, 2014, table 7 (http://www.census.gov/housing/hvs/files/currenthvs press.pdf).

57. Debbie Gruenstein Bocian, Wei Li, Carolina Reid, and Roberto G. Quercia, *Lost Ground, 2011: Disparities in Mortgage Lending and Foreclosures* (Durham, NC: Center for Responsible Lending, 2011) (http://www.responsiblelending.org/mortgage-lending/research -analysis/Lost-Ground-2011.pdf).

58. U.S. Census Bureau, "Net Worth and Asset Ownership of Households: 1998 and 2000," *Current Population Reports: Household*

Studies, May 2003, p. 12. On housing and the black-white gap, see Thomas M. Shapiro, *The Hidden Cost of Being African American: How Wealth Perpetuates Inequality* (New York: Oxford University Press, 2004), pp. 119–122; and generally, Dalton Conley, *Being Black, Living in the Red: Race, Wealth, and Social Policy in America* (Berkeley and Los Angeles: University of California Press, 1999); Oliver and Shapiro, *Black Wealth, White Wealth*; Darrick Hamilton and William Darity Jr., "Race, Wealth, and Intergenerational Poverty," *American Prospect On-Line*, August 19, 2009 (http://www.prospect.org/cs /articles?article=race_wealth_and_intergenerational_poverty).

59. Rakesh Kochhar, Richard Fry, and Paul Taylor, "Twenty-to-One: Wealth Gaps Rise to Record Highs Between Whites, Blacks and Hispanics" (Pew Research Center, Social and Demographic Trends, July 26, 2011) (http://www.pewsocialtrends.org/files/2011/07/SDT -Wealth-Report_7-26-11_FINAL.pdf).

60. Thomas Shapiro, Tatjana Meschede, and Sam Osoro, "The Roots of the Widening Racial Wealth Gap: Explaining the Black-White Economic Divide" (Institute on Assets and Social Policy, Brandeis University, Research and Policy Brief, February 2013) (http://iasp .brandeis.edu/pdfs/Author/shapiro-thomas-m/racialwealthgapbrief .pdf).

61. David A. Hollinger, "Obama, the Instability of Color Lines, and the Promise of a Postethnic Future," *Callaloo* 31 (2008): 1033–1037. For a detailed and optimistic discussion of interracial marriage, see William H. Frey, *Diversity Explosion: How New Racial Demographics Are Remaking America* (Washington, DC: Brookings Institution, 2014), pp. 191–211.

62. Michelle Alexander, *The New Jim Crow: Mass Incarceration in the Age of Colorblindness* (New York: New Press, 2010).

63. Tienda and Fuentes, "Hispanics in Metropolitan America," p. 515.

64. Eduardo Bonilla-Silva, "Are the Americas 'Sick with Racism' or Is It a Problem at the Poles?" *Ethnic and Racial Studies* 32 (2009): 1071– 1082. For other discussions of the issue, see Thomas J. Sugrue, *Not Even Past: Barack Obama and the Burden of Race* (Princeton, NJ: Princeton University Press, 2010), chapter 3; and Daniel T. Lichter, "Integration or Fragmentation? Racial Diversity and the American Future," *Demography* 50 (2013): 359–391.

Chapter 2: Toward a Connected Society

1. Thomas Sugrue (chapter 1 in this volume) provides a good overview of those demographic transitions.

2. This point is underscored by Sugrue in chapter 1: "The color of America will certainly change by 2040, but the meaning of race and ethnicity in the future will depend to a great extent on policy decisions made today."

3. Danielle Allen, "A False Conflict between Liberty and Equality," *Washington Post*, October 26, 2014.

4. For an articulation of these commitments, see Danielle Allen, "Talent Is Everywhere: Using Zip Codes and Merit to Enhance Diversity," in *Beyond Affirmative Action*, ed. R. Kahlenberg (New York: Century Foundation, 2014); Danielle Allen, *Our Declaration: A Reading of the Declaration of Independence in Defense of Equality* (New York: Norton/Liveright, 2014); and Danielle Allen and Jennifer Light, eds., *From Voice to Influence: Understanding Citizenship in a Digital Age* (Chicago: University of Chicago Press, 2015). See the latter also for a brief genealogy of this view and a bibliography.

5. M. S. Katz, "A History of Compulsory Education Laws" (Fastback Series, no. 75, Bicentennial Series, Phi Delta Kappa, 1976). See also C. Goldin and L. Katz, *The Race between Education and Technology* (Cambridge, MA: Belknap Press, 2008).

6. Arthur Schlesinger, *The Disuniting of America: Reflections on a Multicultural Society* (New York: Norton, 1992), pp. 32–33.

7. Ibid., p. 19. The quotation continues thus: "Racism, as I have noted, has been the great national tragedy. . . . When old-line Americans, for example, treat people of other nationalities and races as if they were indigestible elements to be shunned and barred, they must not be surprised if minorities gather bitterly unto themselves and damn everybody else. Not only must *they* want assimilation and integration; *we* must want assimilation and integration too."

8. Angel Parham, "Who Are We? What Louisiana Can Teach Us about Being American" (Occasional Paper no. 44, School of Social Science at the Institute for Advanced Study, 2012) (http://www.sss.ias.edu /publications/occasional).

9. Experience of Carola Suárez-Orozco as narrated to author by Marcelo Suárez-Orozco, October 6, 2014.

10. R. Ellison, *Invisible Man* (New York: Vintage, 1980 [originally published 1952]), p. 557.

11. This commission was charged "to recommend what steps should be taken to develop the Canadian Confederation on the basis of an equal partnership between the two founding races [French and English], taking into account the contribution made by the other ethnic groups to the cultural enrichment of Canada and the measures that should be taken to safeguard that contribution." "Report of the

Royal Commission on Bilingualism and Biculturalism" (A. Davidson Dunton, Co-Chairman; Andre Laurendeau, Co-Chairman), general introduction, p. xxi (http://epe.lac-bac.gc.ca/100/200/301/pco-bcp /commissions-ef/dunton1967-1970-ef/dunton1967-70-eng.htm). In 1971, following on the work of this commission, the Canadian federal government decided to pursue a policy of multiculturalism, not biculturalism. Eventually, in the early 1980s it enshrined particular multicultural rights—for instance, language rights—in an amended constitution. Constitution Act 1982 (Canada) (http:// www.solon.org/Constitutions/Canada/English/ca_1982.html).

12. Charles Taylor, *Multiculturalism: Examining the Politics of Recognition* (Princeton, NJ: Princeton University Press, 1994). Taylor's powerful essay was supplemented by comments from other philosophers, among them K. Anthony Appiah, Jürgen Habermas, and Michael Walzer, and the volume was quickly translated into Italian, French, and German, thus launching "multiculturalism" as a fully multinational subject of exploration and policy development.

13. Schlesinger, *The Disuniting of America*, pp. 17–18. The 1993 dissolution of Czechoslovakia into two nations, the Czech Republic and Slovakia, each encompassing a distinct linguistic and ethnic group, was a case in point, as was the subsequent disintegration of Yugoslavia.

14. Homi Bhabha, *The Location of Culture* (New York: Routledge, 1994).

15. Homi Bhabha, "Cultural Diversity and Cultural Differences," in *Atlas of Transformation*, ed. Zbynek Baladrán and Vit Havránek (2011) (http://monumenttotransformation.org/atlas-of-transforma tion/html/c/cultural-diversity/cultural-diversity-and-cultural-differ ences-homi-k-bhabha.html, accessed January 21, 2015).

16. Iris M. Young, "Gender as Seriality: Thinking about Women as a Social Collective," *Signs* 19, no. 3 (1994): 713–738.

17. Cf. Walter Benn Michaels, *The Trouble with Diversity: How We Learned to Love Identity and Ignore Inequality* (New York: Henry Holt, 2007).

18. Regents of the University of California v. Bakke, 438 U.S. 265 (1978): 313.

19. Grutter v. Bollinger, 539 U.S. 306 (2003).

20. Parents Involved in Community Schools v. Seattle School District No. 1, 551 U.S. at 748 (2007).

21. Lionel K. McPherson, "Righting Historical Injustice in Higher Education," in *The Aims of Higher Education: Problems of Morality*

and Justice, ed. M. McPherson and H. Brighouse (Chicago: University of Chicago Press, 2015).

22. Ibid.

23. Marcelo Suárez-Orozco and Mariela Páez, *Latinos: Remaking America* (Berkeley and Los Angeles: University of California Press, 2008).

24. UC Berkeley Strategic Plan for Equity, Inclusion, and Diversity 2009, p. 5 (http://diversity.berkeley.edu/guiding-principles-excellence-equity -and-inclusion and http://diversity.berkeley.edu/sites/default/files /ExecutiveSummary_webversion.pdf).

25. Bernard Bailyn, *The Barbarous Years: The Peopling of British North America—The Conflict of Civilizations, 1600–1675* (New York: Vintage Books, 2013).

26. New York City Department of Education, Office of English Language Learners, "2013 Demographic Report, New York City Department of Education, Division of Students with Disabilities and English Language Learners" (2013) (http://schools.nyc.gov/NR /rdonlyres/FD5EB945–5C27–44F8-BE4B-E4C65D7176F8/0/2013 DemographicReport_june2013_revised.pdf, accessed January 22, 2015).

27. Robert Putnam and David Campbell, *American Grace: How Religion Divides and Unites Us* (New York: Simon & Schuster, 2010).

28. D. Smith et al., "The Pipeline for Achieving Faculty Diversity: Debunking the Myths" (Association for the Study of Higher Education, 1996) (http://www.eric.ed.gov/ERICWebPortal/search/de tailmini.jsp?_nfpb=true&_&ERICExtSearch_SearchValue_0=ED4 02836&ERICExtSearch_SearchType_0=no&accno=ED402836); J. Moreno et al., "The Revolving Door for Underrepresented Minority Faculty in Higher Education" (Association of American Colleges and Universities, 2006) (https://folio.iupui.edu/bitstream/handle /10244/50/insight_Revolving_Door.pdf?sequence=1).

29. http://opa.berkeley.edu/uc-berkeley-fall-enrollment-data (2013); Stanford Facts 2014, p. 13 (http://facts.stanford.edu/pdf/Stanford-Facts_2014.pdf).

30. http://www.huffingtonpost.com/2013/11/08/ucla-black-enrollment -freshmen_n_4242213.html.

31. See n. 24.

32. There is extensive literature on this subject.

33. Danielle Allen, "A Connected Society," *Soundings* 53 (Spring 2013): 103–113.

34. Marc S. Granovetter, "The Strength of Weak Ties," *American Journal of Sociology* 78 (1973): 1360–1380; S. Szreter and M.

Woolcock, "Health by Association? Social Capital, Social Theory, and the Political Economy of Public Health," *International Journal of Epidemiology* 33, no. 4 (2004): 650–667.

35. For instance, J. Ober, *Democracy and Knowledge* (Princeton, NJ: Princeton University Press, 2008); Szreter and Woolcock, "Health by Association?"

36. Granovetter, "The Strength of Weak Ties."

37. For the economy, the benefits of a connected society include:

—Improvements in education because of a broader diffusion of the linguistic, intellectual, and social resources that support learning in the first place as well as impacts on personal decisions about whether to invest in education (Matthew O. Jackson, "Social Structure, Segregation, and Economic Behavior" [presented as the Nancy Schwartz Memorial Lecture, April 2007; revised, February 5, 2009, http://papers.ssrn.com/abstract=1530885]; A. Lareau, *Unequal Childhoods: Class, Race, and Family Life*, 2nd ed. [Berkeley and Los Angeles: University of California Press, 2011]; J. Ludwig, H. F. Ladd, and G. J. Duncan, "Urban Poverty and Educational Outcomes," *Brookings-Wharton Papers on Urban Affairs* 200 [2001]: 147–201);

—Increases to social mobility because a better diffusion of information allows people to see opportunities and fit themselves to them (Granovetter, "The Strength of Weak Ties"; Jackson, "Social Structure, Segregation, and Economic Behavior");

—Increases to creativity because diverse solution approaches are more likely to be brought into conversation with one another (Scott E. Page, *The Difference: How the Power of Diversity Creates Better Groups, Firms, Schools, and Societies* [Princeton, NJ: Princeton University Press, 2007]);

—More efficient knowledge transmission because information travels faster across bridging connections (Granovetter, "The Strength of Weak Ties"; Jackson, "Social Structure, Segregation, and Economic Behavior").

For democratic politics, the benefits of a connected society include:

—Improved social awareness and public discourse because citizens have more exposure to the impacts on others of different policy questions and, with improved information flows across social ties, citizens are less likely to consider the beliefs of others to be simply incorrect (Rajiv Sethi and Muhamet Yildiz, "Public

Disagreement," *American Economic Journal: Microeconomics* 4, no. 3 [2012]: 57–95);

—More efficient policy planning because policy makers can more easily draw on local knowledge to ensure alignment of policies with on-the-ground realities (Ober, *Democracy and Knowledge*);

—The creation of "latent publics" because social connections across communities help communities discover new kinds of alliances (John Dewey, *The Public and Its Problems*, ed. Melvin Rogers [University Park: Pennsylvania State University Press, 2012; originally published 1927]);

—A background cultural expectation of connectedness that sets into even sharper relief "disconnected," "out-of-touch" policy approaches, such as that used by the Tories when they developed National Health Service reform without consultation with the holders of local knowledge.

For personal well-being, the benefits of a connected society include:

—An increased sense of agency because of access to a larger opportunity network (Danielle Allen, *Talking to Strangers* [Chicago: University of Chicago Press, 2004]);

—Increased opportunity to develop important relational skills, not merely those that support the intimacy of bonding relationships, but also the skills of the interpreter, mediator, and greeter, which serve to build and use bridging relationships (Allen, *Talking to Strangers*);

—The opportunity to protect and enjoy one's own culture without falling into isolation (J. Sidanius, S. Levin, C. van Laar, and D. O. Sears, *The Diversity Challenge: Social Identity and Intergroup Relations on the College Campus* [New York: Russell Sage Foundation, 2008]).

For the general benefits of egalitarianism, see Kate Pickett and Richard Wilkinson, *The Spirit Level: Why Greater Equality Makes Societies Stronger* (New York: Bloomsbury Press, 2011).

38. Glenn C. Loury, "A Dynamic Theory of Racial Income Differences," in *Women, Minorities and Employment Discrimination*, ed. Phyllis Wallace and Annette LaMond (Lexington, MA: Lexington Books, 1977); Glenn C. Loury, *The Anatomy of Racial Inequality* (Cambridge, MA: Harvard University Press, 2002); Elizabeth Anderson, *The Imperative of Integration* (Princeton, NJ: Princeton University Press, 2010); R. Rothstein, "Racial Segregation and Black Student

Achievement," in *Education, Justice, and Democracy*, ed. Danielle Allen and Rob Reich (Chicago: University of Chicago Press, 2013), pp. 173–198.

39. Samuel Bowles, Glenn C. Loury, and Rajiv Sethi, "Group Inequality," *Journal of the European Economic Association* (forthcoming) (http://www.columbia.edu/~rs328/GroupInequality.pdf, accessed January 22, 2015).

40. Anderson, *The Imperative of Integration*.

41. Lareau, *Unequal Childhoods*.

42. Ibid.

43. Ober, *Democracy and Knowledge*; Szreter and Woolcock, "Health by Association?"

44. Jacob Hacker, "The Institutional Foundations of Middle-Class Democracy" (Policy Network, 2011) (http://www.policy-network.net /pno_detail.aspx?ID=3998&title=The+institutional+foundations +of+middle-class+democracy).

45. D. Kirp, "The Benefits of Mixing Rich and Poor," *New York Times*, May 10, 2014 (http://opinionator.blogs.nytimes.com/2014/05/10 /the-benefits-of-mixing-rich-and-poor/?_r=0#more-152970).

46. M. Reich and K. Jacobs, "All Economics Is Local," *New York Times*, March 22, 2014 (http://opinionator.blogs.nytimes.com/2014/03/22 /all-economics-is-local/#more-152533).

47. R. Sampson, "Division Street, U.S.A.," *New York Times*, October 23, 2013 (http://opinionator.blogs.nytimes.com/2013/10/26/division -street-u-s-a/#more-150124); see also R. Rothstein, "If the Supreme Court Bans the Disparate Impact Standard It Could Annihilate One of the Few Tools Available to Pursue Housing Integration" (Economic Policy Institute, January 2015) (http://www.epi.org/publication /if-the-supreme-court-bans-the-disparate-impact-standard-it-could -annihilate-one-of-the-few-tools-available-to-pursue-housing-integra tion/).

48. Heather Gerken, "The Loyal Opposition," *Yale Law Journal* 123 (2014): 1958–1994.

49. Allen, "Talent Is Everywhere."

50. P. Bourdieu, "The Forms of Capital," in *Handbook of Theory and Research for the Sociology of Education*, ed. J. Richardson (Westport, CT: Greenwood Press, 1986); J. Coleman, "Social Capital in the Creation of Human Capital," *American Journal of Sociology* 94 (1988): S95–120; Robert D. Putnam, *Making Democracy Work: Civic Traditions in Modern Italy* (Princeton, NJ: Princeton University Press, 1993); Robert D. Putnam, *Bowling Alone: The Collapse*

and Revival of American Community (New York: Touchstone, 2000).

51. Putnam, *Bowling Alone*, pp. 21–22.
52. Robert D. Putnam, "*E Pluribus Unum*: Diversity and Community in the Twenty-first Century," *Scandinavian Political Studies* 30, no. 2 (2007): 137–174.
53. Ibid., p. 164. This (the 2006 Johan Skytte Prize Lecture) presents findings from the Social Capital Community Benchmark Survey, "the largest and most comprehensive survey of civic engagement in America." "The survey results revealed that Americans who live in more ethnically diverse communities are less likely to vote, do volunteer work, and trust others (both of the same and of different ethnicities / races) than are those who live in more ethnically homogenous communities. In other words, higher levels of ethnic and racial diversity are related to lower levels of civic health." http://prelectur.stanford.edu/lecturers/putnam/. Text by Chris Bourg, Assistant University Librarian for Public Services. Stanford University Libraries & Academic Information Resources © 2010.
54. Page, *The Difference*; Mary M. Maloney and Mary Zellmer-Bruhn, "Building Bridges, Windows and Cultures: Mediating Mechanisms between Team Heterogeneity and Performance in Global Teams," *MIR: Management International Review* 46, no. 6 (December 2006): 697–720; Astrid C. Homan, John R. Hollenbeck, Stephen E. Humphrey, Daan Van Knippenberg, Daniel R. Ilgen, and Gerben A. Van Kleef, "Facing Differences with an Open Mind: Openness to Experience, Salience of Intragroup Differences, and Performance of Diverse Work Groups," *Academy of Management Journal* 51, no. 6 (December 2008): 1204–1222. See also Anthony Carnevale and Nicole Smith (chapter 3 in this volume) on the relationship among diversity, innovation, and economic benefit.
55. M. Ferguson, *Sharing Democracy* (Oxford: Oxford University Press, 2012).
56. Homan et al., "Facing Differences with an Open Mind."
57. Ibid.; Maloney and Zellmer-Bruhn, "Building Bridges, Windows and Cultures."
58. "Specifically, we propose that structural and procedural features can be combined and manipulated to mitigate the potential problems associated with heterogeneity and distance, and more importantly, to enhance the likelihood that the benefits are realized." Maloney and Zellmer-Bruhn, "Building Bridges, Windows and Cultures," p. 705.
59. Ibid.

60. In conditions of mismatch, it's important that people be prepared to create "swift norms": ibid.

61. I have made this argument in an extended fashion in an unpublished paper, "The Art of Association," which tracks the changes in the law of association between 1970 and 1990 and the impacts of those legal changes on the social organizations in which Putnam is interested. The research is ongoing. The hypothesis of the research is that as the changed legal landscape demanded gender integration, the clubs suffered because the knowledge that they had inculcated in club members did not serve them well in the context of gender and racial integration. This means, though, that the problem affecting the clubs was, contra to the explanations offered by Putnam, their failure to adapt out bodies of social knowledge to new legal and institutional landscapes that had, appropriately, evolved in a more democratic direction. I am currently working with Bob Lowry (University of Texas–Dallas) to test this hypothesis.

62. Maloney and Zellmer-Bruhn, "Building Bridges, Windows and Cultures"; Homan et al., "Facing Differences with an Open Mind."

63. P. M. Bromberg, *The Shadow of the Tsunami and the Growth of the Relational Mind* (New York: Routledge, 2011); A. Honneth, "Integrity and Disrespect: Principles of a Conception of Morality Based on a Theory of Recognition," *Political Theory* 20, no. 2 (1992): 187–201.

64. Sidanius et al., *The Diversity Challenge.*

65. Bromberg, *The Shadow of the Tsunami and the Growth of the Relational Mind.*

66. Anderson, *The Imperative of Integration.*

67. Some answers to this question can be found in the psychological literature, for instance, a stress on the "openness to experience" factor in the five-factor model of personality (R. R. McCrae and P. T. Costa, "Validation of the Five Factor Model of Personality across Instruments and Observers," *Journal of Personality and Social Psychology* 52 [1987]: 81–90) in Homan et al., "Facing Differences with an Open Mind"; and "a global mindset" in Maloney and Zellmer-Bruhn, "Building Bridges, Windows and Cultures."

68. Allen, *Our Declaration.*

Chapter 3: The Economic Value of Diversity

1. Robert D. Putnam, "*E Pluribus Unum:* Diversity and Community in the Twenty-first Century," *Scandinavian Political Studies* 30 (2007): 137–174 (http://onlinelibrary.wiley.com/doi/10.1111/j.1467-9477

.2007.00176.x/pdf); M. Yuki, W. W. Maddux, M. B. Brewer, and K. Takemura, "Cross-Cultural Differences in Relationships—and Group-Based Trust," *Personality and Social Psychology Bulletin* 31 (2005): 48–62 (http://dx.doi.10.1177/0146167204271305); W. A. Cunningham, J. B. Nezlek, and M. R. Banaji, "Implicit and Explicit Ethnocentrism: Revisiting the Ideologies of Prejudice," *Society for Personality and Social Psychology* 30 (2004): 1332–1346 (http://dx.10.1177/0146167204264654).

2. Anthony P. Carnevale and Stephen J. Rose, "The Economy Goes to College: The Hidden Promise of Higher Education in the Post-Industrial Service Economy" (Georgetown University Center for Education and the Workforce [hereafter, CEW], 2015) (https://cew.georgetown.edu/report/economygoestocollege/).

3. Ibid.

4. Ibid.

5. Ibid.

6. Ibid.

7. Ibid.

8. Christopher Hill, "The Post-Scientific Society," *Issues in Science and Technology*, Fall 2007 (http://www.issues.org/24.1/c_hill.html).

9. Phillip Ager and Markus Brückner, "Cultural Diversity and Economic Growth: Evidence from the US during the Age of Mass Migration," *European Economic Review* 64 (2013): 76–97.

10. Giancarmo Ottaviano and Giovanni Peri, "The Economic Value of Cultural Diversity: Evidence from US Cities," *Journal of Economic Geography* 6 (2006): 9–44 (http://joeg.oxfordjournals.org/content/6/1/9.full.pdf+html).

11. Chad Sparber, "Racial Diversity and Macroeconomic Productivity across US States and Cities," *Regional Studies* 44 (2010): 71–85 (http://www.colgate.edu/portaldata/imagegallerywww/0225a1d8-0850-4bb1-88f2-fc550662e306/ImageGallery/macro.pdf).

12. Cedric Herring, "Does Diversity Pay? Race, Gender, and the Business Case for Diversity," *American Sociological Review* 74 (2009): 208–224 (http://www.asanet.org/images/journals/docs/pdf/asr/Apr09ASR Feature.pdf).

13. Deloitte, Inc., "Only Skin Deep? Re-examining the Business Case for Diversity" (2011) (https://www.ced.org/pdf/Deloitte_-_Only_Skin_Deep.pdf).

14. R. Ostergaard, Bram Timmermans, and Kari Kristinsson. "Does a Different View Create Something New? The Effect of Employee Diversity on Innovation," *Research Policy* 40, no. 3 (2011): 500–509 (http://www.sciencedirect.com/science/article/pii/S00487333

10002398); Pierpaolo Parrotta, Dario Pozzoli, and Mariola Pytlikova, "The Nexus between Labor Diversity and Firm's Innovation," *Journal of Population Economics* 27 (2014): 303–364 (http://www.norface-migration.org/publ_uploads/NDP_05_11.pdf).

15. Orlando C. Richard, "Racial Diversity, Business Strategy, and Firm Performance: A Resource-Based View," *Academy of Management Journal* 43 (2000): 164–177 (http://www.jstor.org/discover/10.230 7/1556374?uid=3739704&uid=2134&uid=2&uid=70&uid=4&u id=3739256&sid=21104864575027).

16. Orlando C. Richard, B.P.S. Murthi, and Kiran Ismail, "The Impact of Racial Diversity on Intermediate and Long-term Performance: The Moderating Role of Environmental Context," *Strategic Management Journal* 28 (2007): 1213–1233 (http://onlinelibrary.wiley.com/doi/10 .1002/smj.633/abstract).

17. Catalyst, "The Bottom Line: Connecting Corporate Performance and Gender Diversity" (2004) (http://www.catalyst.org/knowledge /bottom-line-connecting-corporate-performance-and-gender-diversity).

18. Catalyst, "The Bottom Line: Corporate Performance and Women's Representation on Boards" (2007) (http://www.catalyst.org/knowledge/ bottom-line-corporate-performance-and-womens-representation -boards).

19. Deloitte, "Only Skin Deep?"

20. Lu Hong and Scott E. Page, "Groups of Diverse Problem Solvers Can Outperform Groups of High-Ability Problem Solvers," *Proceedings of the National Academy of Sciences (PNAS)* 101 (2004): 16385–16389 (http://www.pnas.org/content/101/46/16385.full.pdf+html).

21. Scott E. Page, *The Difference: How the Power of Diversity Creates Better Groups, Firms, Schools, and Societies* (Princeton, NJ: Princeton University Press, 2007).

22. Karen A. Jehn, Gregory B. Northcraft, and Margaret A. Neale, "Why Differences Make a Difference: A Field Study of Diversity, Conflict and Performance in Workgroups," *Administrative Science Quarterly* 44 (1999): 741–763; Page, *The Difference*.

23. Richard B. Freeman and Wei Huang, "Collaborating with People Like Me: Ethnic Co-Authorship within the US" (NBER Working Paper No. 19905, 2014) (http://www.nber.org/papers/w19905).

24. Discussion of the Diversity Prediction Theorem in Page, *The Difference*, chapter 8.

25. Page, *The Difference*.

26. Marie-Elène Roberge and Rolf van Dick, "Recognizing the Benefits of Diversity: When and How Does Diversity Increase Group

Performance?" *Human Resource Management Review* 20 (2010): 295–308.

27. Wanda T. Wallace and Gillian Pillans, *Diversity and Business Performance* (London: Corporate Research Forum, 2011).

28. Marcus Robinson, Charles Pfeffer, and Joan Buccigrossi, "Business Case for Diversity with Inclusion" (WetWare, Inc., 2003) (http://workforcediversitynetwork.com/docs/business_case_3.pdf).

29. Jeffrey M. Humphreys, *The Multicultural Economy* (Athens: University of Georgia, 2013).

30. Wallace and Pillans, *Diversity and Business Performance*.

31. Patricia Gurin, Biren (Ratnesh) A. Nagda, and Ximena Zúñiga, *Dialogue across Difference: Practice, Theory, and Research on Intergroup Dialogue* (New York: Russell Sage Foundation, 2013).

32. Sean F. Reardon, Elena Grewal, Demetra Kalogrides, and Erica Greenberg, "Brown Fades: The End of Court-Ordered School Desegregation and the Resegregation of American Public Schools," *Journal of Policy Analysis and Management* 31, no. 4 (2012): 876–904.

33. "Secretary Duncan, Urban League President Morial to Spotlight States Where Education Funding Shortchanges Low-Income, Minority Students" (Education Finance Statistics Center, National Center on Education Statistics, March 2015) (http://nces.ed.gov/edfin/xls/A-1_FY2012.xls).

34. Georgetown University Center on Education and the Workforce analysis, using U.S. Census Bureau and Bureau of Labor Statistics, *Current Population Survey*, March Supplement (Washington, DC: U.S. Census Bureau and Bureau of Labor Statistics, 2013) (https://www.census.gov/hhes/www/poverty/publications/pubs-cps.html), and Anthony P. Carnevale, Stephen J. Rose, and Ban Cheah, "The College Payoff: Education, Occupations, Lifetime Earnings" (Georgetown University Center on Education and the Workforce, 2011) (http://cew.georgetown.edu/collegepayoff).

35. David Autor, "Skills, Education, and the Rise of Earnings Inequality among the 'Other 99 Percent,'" *Science* 344 (2014): 843–851.

36. Anthony P. Carnevale and Stephen J. Rose, "The Undereducated American" (Georgetown University Center on Education and the Workforce, 2012) (https://cew.georgetown.edu/undereducated).

37. Christopher Jencks and Meredith Phillips, *The Black-White Test Score Gap* (Washington, DC: Brookings Institution Press, 1998).

38. Rackesh Kochar, Richard Fry, and Paul Taylor, "Wealth Gaps Rise to Record Highs between Whites, Blacks and Hispanics" (Pew Research

Center, 2011) (http://www.pewsocialtrends.org/files/2011/07/SDT
-Wealth-Report_7-26-11_FINAL.pdf).

39. Jencks and Phillips, *The Black-White Test Score Gap*, p. 2.
40. This study is based in part on a three-year pooled Integrated Post-secondary Education Data System (IPEDS) sample; hence the number of schools is approximate. Data are pooled to smooth small annual fluctuations in freshman enrollment.
41. John R. Logan, "Separate and Unequal in Suburbia" (Census Brief prepared for Project US2010, 2014) (http://www.s4.brown.edu/us 2010/Data/Report/report12012014.pdf).
42. Anthony P. Carnevale and Jeff Strohl, "Separate and Unequal" (CEW, 2013) (http://cew.georgetown.edu/separateandunequal).
43. U.S. Department of Education, Institute of Education Sciences, National Center for Education Statistics, *Digest of Education Statistics*, table 326.10 (2011–2012 data), 2013 (http://nces.ed.gov/programs /digest/d13/tables/dt13_326.10.asp).
44. CEW analysis of U.S. Census Bureau statistics, "America's Families," table C3.
45. U.S. Department of Education, Institute of Education Sciences, National Center for Education Statistics, *National Assessment of Educational Progress (NAEP)*, 2013 (http://nces.ed.gov/nationsreportcard/).
46. U.S. Department of Education, Institute of Education Sciences, National Center for Education Statistics, *Digest of Education Statistics*, table 125 (2009–2010 data), 2012 (http://nces.ed.gov/programs /digest/d12/tables/dt12_125.asp).
47. CEW analysis of U.S. Department of Education, Institute of Education Sciences, National Center for Education Statistics, *Digest of Education Statistics*, table 226.10 (2011–2012 data), 2013 (http:// nces.ed.gov/programs/digest/d13/tables/dt13_226.10.asp).
48. CEW analysis of U.S. Census, *Current Population Survey*, 2013.
49. Albeit a new normal, characterized by an increase in the natural rate of unemployment (William T. Dickens, "Has the Recession Increased the NAIRU?" [Northeastern University and Brookings Institution Working Paper, 2011, http://www.brookings.edu/~/media/research /files/papers/2011/6/29%20recession%20nairu%20dickens/0629 _recession_nairu_dickens.pdf]; Robert Gordon, "The Phillips Curve Is Alive and Well: Inflation and the NAIRU during the Slow Recovery" [NBER Working Papers, no. 19390, National Bureau of Economic Research, 2013, http://www.nber.org/papers/w19390]), lower labor force participation (Shigeru Fujita, "On the Causes of Declines in the Labor Force Participation Rate" [Special Report, Research

Rap, Federal Reserve Bank of Philadelphia, 2014, http://philadelphi-afed.org/research-and-data/publications/research-rap/2013/on-the-causes-of-declines-in-the-labor-force-participation-rate.pdf]), perma-nent job losses in sectors employing the less-educated, and an ever-increasing demand for better education credentials and upskilling across an array of new fields (Anthony P. Carnevale and Nicole Smith, "Recovery: Job Growth and Education Requirements through 2020" [CEW, 2013, http://cew.georgetown.edu/recovery2020]).

50. CEW analysis of U.S. Department of Education, *Digest of Educa-tion Statistics*, table 321.30.

51. CEW analysis of *Current Population Survey*, March Supplement, 1980.

52. CEW projection of labor force makeup by race/ethnicity, 2014.

53. D'Vera Cohn and Paul Taylor, "Baby Boomers Approach 65—Glumly: Survey Findings about America's Largest Genera-tion" (Pew Research Center, 2010) (http://www.pewsocialtrends.org/2010/12/20/baby-boomers-approach-65-glumly/).

54. Starlene M. Simons and Kimberly M. Rowland, "Diversity and Its Impact on Organizational Performance: The Influence of Diversity Constructions on Expectations and Outcomes," *Journal of Technol-ogy, Management and Innovation* 6 (2011): 71–183 (http://www.scielo.cl/pdf/jotmi/v6n3/art13.pdf); Julie Christian, Lyman W. Por-ter, and Graham Moffitt, "Workplace Diversity and Group Rela-tions: An Overview," *Group Processes and Intergroup Relations* 9 (2006): 459–466 (http://www.sagepub.com/zibarras/study/Chapter%204/Group%20Processes%20Intergroup%20Relations-2006-Christian-459-66.pdf); Marlene G. Fine, "Cultural Diversity in the Workplace: The State of the Field," *Journal of Business Com-munication* 33 (1996): 485–502.

55. Taylor Cox Jr., "The Multicultural Organization," *Academy of Management Executive* 5 (1991): 34–47 (http://www.jstor.org/disco ver/10.2307/4165006?uid=3739704&uid=2&uid=4&uid=3739256 &sid=21104864575027).

56. Sparber, "Racial Diversity and Macroeconomic Productivity across US States and Cities."

57. J. S. Bunderson and K. M. Sutcliffe, "Comparing Alternative Con-ceptualizations of Functional Diversity in Management Teams," *Academy of Management Journal* 45 (2002): 875–893.

58. Kenneth A. Couch and Robert Fairlie, "Last Hired, First Fired? Black-White Unemployment and the Business Cycle," *Demography* 47 (2010): 227–247.

59. Claudia Goldin and Lawrence F. Katz, *The Race between Education and Technology* (Cambridge, MA: Belknap Press, 2010).

60. John Cohen and Dan Balz, "Poll: Whites without College Degrees Especially Pessimistic about Economy," *Washington Post*, February 22, 2011 (http://www.washingtonpost.com/wp-dyn/content/article/2011/02/22/AR2011022200005.html?nav=emailpage).

61. Jesse M. Rothstein, "College Performance Predictions and the SAT," *Journal of Econometrics* 121 (2004): 297–317 (http://gsppi.berkeley.edu/faculty/jrothstein/published/sat_may03_updated.pdf).

62. Carnevale and Strohl, "Separate and Unequal."

63. Author's calculations based on U.S. Census Bureau, *Current Population Survey*, 1980–2010.

64. Claudia Goldin and Lawrence F. Katz, "Long-Run Changes in the U.S Wage Structure: Narrowing, Widening, Polarizing" (Working Paper No. 13568, National Bureau of Economic Research, 2007) (http://www.nber.org/papers/w13568).

65. See, for example, Robert J. Gordon, *The Rise and Fall of American Growth: The U.S. Standard of Living since the Civil War* (Princeton, NJ: Princeton University Press, 2016).

66. Alfred Marshall, cited in *Memorials of Alfred Marshall*, ed. A. C. Pigou (London: Macmillan, 1925), p. 102.

67. T. H. Marshall, "Citizenship and Social Class," in *Contemporary Political Philosophy: An Anthology*, ed. R. E. Goodin and P. Pettit (Oxford: Blackwell, 1997), p. 311.

68. Heather Hahn, Julia Isaacs, Sarah Edelstein, Ellen Steele, and E. Eugene Steuerle, "Kids' Share 2014: Report on Federal Expenditures on Children through 2013" (Urban Institute, 2013) (http://www.urban.org/UploadedPDF/413215-Kids-Share-2014.pdf).

69. Grayson K. Vincent and Victoria A. Velkoff, "The Next Four Decades: The Older Population in the United States: 2010 to 2050" (U.S. Census Bureau, 2010) (http://www.census.gov/prod/2010pubs/p25-1138.pdf).

70. Vanessa Cárdenas, Julie Ajinkya, and Daniella Gibbs Léger, "Progress 2050: New Ideas for a Diverse America" (Center for American Progress, October 2011) (http://cdn.americanprogress.org/wp-content/uploads/issues/2011/10/pdf/progress_2050.pdf).

71. The seminal work of Eric Turkheimer and his team at the University of Virginia shows that for most low-income kids there is no relationship between innate abilities measured in childhood and aptitudes developed by the time they are old enough for college. In other words, if you come from a poor or working-poor family,

chances are you won't be able to "be all you can be." At worst, these children are not only isolated geographically, oftentimes in our urban free-fire zones, but also isolated from the American dream. With no way out, they don't live in America; they live underneath America. Conversely, students from affluent families are much more likely to become all they can be in the transitions between childhood, college, and careers. Turkheimer and his team find that test scores of affluent children when they are young are good predictors of their developed abilities when it's time to apply to college.

72. James J. Heckman, "What Should Be Our Human Capital Investment Policy?" *Fiscal Studies* 19 (1998): 103–119 (http://onlinelibrary.wiley .com/doi/10.1111/j.1475-5890.1998.tb00279.x/references).

73. Clive R. Belfield, Henry M. Levin, and Rachel Rosen, "The Economic Value of Opportunity Youth" (Corporation for National and Community Service, 2012) (http://www.civicenterprises.net/Media Library/Docs/econ_value_opportunity_youth.pdf).

74. CEW analysis using U.S. Census Bureau *Current Population Survey*, 2013, and Carnevale, Rose, and Cheah, "The College Payoff."

75. Lawrence J. Schweinhart, Jeanne Montie, Zongping Xiang, W. Steven Barnett, Clive R. Belfield, and Milagros Nores, *Lifetime Effects: The High/Scope Perry Preschool Study through Age 40* (Ypsilanti, MI: High/Scope Press, 2005).

76. See http://www.npr.org/blogs/money/2011/08/12/139583385/pre school-the-best-job-training-program.

77. James J. Heckman, "The Case for Investing in Disadvantaged Young Children," in *Big Ideas for Children: Investing in Our Nation's Future* (Washington, DC: First Focus, 2008) (http://heckmanequation. org/download.php?file=Heckman$$$Investing$$$in$$$Young$$$ Children.pdf).

78. See http://www.npr.org/blogs/money/2011/08/12/139583385/pre school-the-best-job-training-program.

79. Pew Center on the States, *Transforming Public Education: Pathway to a Pre-K–12 Future* (Philadelphia: Pew Charitable Trusts, 2011) (http:// www.pewtrusts.org/en/research-and-analysis/reports/2011/09/26 /transforming-public-education-pathway-to-a-prek12-future).

80. Mary Bruce and John Bridgeland, "The Mentoring Effect: Young People's Perspectives on the Outcomes and Availability of Mentoring" (Civic Enterprises in association with Hart Research Associates, 2014) (http://www.mentoring.org/images/uploads/Report_TheMen toringEffect.pdf).

81. Ibid.

82. Anthony P. Carnevale, Nicole Smith, Michelle Melton, and Eric W. Price, "Learning while Earning: The New Normal" (CEW, 2015) (https://cew.georgetown.edu/wp-content/uploads/Working-Learners -Report.pdf).

83. U.S. Department of Education, "College Ratings and Paying for Performance" (2014) (http://www.ed.gov/college-affordability/college -ratings-and-paying-performance).

84. Ibid.

Chapter 4: The Diversity of Diversity

1. Gary J. Kornblith, "Self-Made Men: The Development of Middling-Class Consciousness in New England," *Massachusetts Review* 26, no. 2/3 (Summer–Autumn 1985): 461–474.

2. George Berkeley, *A Treatise Concerning the Principles of Human Knowledge* (Mineola, NY: Dover Publications, 2003), p. 84.

3. Claude Steele, *Whistling Vivaldi: How Stereotypes Affect Us and What We Can Do* (New York: W. W. Norton, 2011).

4. http://www.reducingstereotypethreat.org/bibliography_ambady _shih_kim_pittinsky.html. Discussion: N. Ambady, M. Shih, A. Kim, and T. L. Pittinsky, "Stereotype Susceptibility in Children: Effects of Identity Activation on Quantitative Performance," *Psychological Science* 12, no. 5 (2001): 385–390.

5. B. Keith Payne, "Weapon Bias: Split-Second Decisions and Unintended Stereotyping," *Current Directions in Psychological Science* 15, no. 6 (2006): 287–291.

6. Anne Cutler and Donia R. Scott, "Speaker Sex and Perceived Apportionment of Talk," *Applied Psycholinguistics* 11 (1990): 253–272 (doi:10.1017/S0142716400008882).

7. Actually, interviews, especially unstructured ones, are a pretty bad tool for job selection anyway. For a recent discussion, see Jason Dana, Robyn Dawes, and Nathanial Peterson, "Belief in the Unstructured Interview: The Persistence of an Illusion," *Judgment and Decision Making* 8, no. 5 (September 2013): 512–520.

8. Scott E. Page, *The Difference: How the Power of Diversity Creates Better Groups, Firms, Schools, and Societies* (Princeton, NJ: Princeton University Press, 2008).

9. David Campbell and Robert D. Putnam, *American Grace: How Religion Divides and Unites Us* (New York: Simon and Schuster, 2012); Thomas Mann and Norm Ornstein, *It's Worse Than It Looks: How the American Constitutional System Collided with the New Politics of Extremism* (New York: Basic Books, 2013).

Chapter 5: Group Interactions in Building a Connected Society

1. James Rosenbaum, Caitlin Ahern, Kelly Becker, and Janet Rosenbaum, *The New Forgotten Half and Research Directions to Support Them* (New York: W. T. Grant Foundation, 2015), quotation on p. 5.

2. Scott E. Page, *The Difference: How the Power of Diversity Creates Better Groups, Firms, Schools, and Societies* (Princeton, NJ: Princeton University Press, 2007); Scott E. Page, *Diversity and Complexity* (Princeton, NJ: Princeton University Press, 2011).

3. Katherine W. Phillips, Gregory B. Northcraft, and Margaret A. Neale, "Surface-Level Diversity and Decision-Making in Groups: When Does Deep-Level Similarity Help?" *Group Processes and Intergroup Relations* 9, no. 4 (2006): 467–482 (doi:10.1177/1368430206067557).

4. Katherine W. Phillips and Denise Lewin Loyd, "When Surface and Deep-Level Diversity Collide: The Effects on Dissenting Group Members," *Organizational Behavior and Human Decision Processes* 99, no. 2 (2006): 143–160.

5. Robert D. Putnam, "*E Pluribus Unum*: Diversity and Community in the Twenty-first Century: The 2006 Johan Skytte Prize Lecture," *Scandinavian Political Studies* 30, no. 2 (2007): 137–174 (doi:10.1111/j.1467-9477.2007.00176.x).

6. See especially Patrick Sturgis, Ian Brunton-Smith, Sanna Read, and Nick Allum, "Does Ethnic Diversity Erode Trust? Putnam's 'Hunkering Down' Thesis Reconsidered," *British Journal of Political Science* 41, no. 1 (2011): 57–82 (doi:10.1017/s0007123410000281).

7. Patricia Gurin, *The Compelling Need for Diversity in Higher Education* (Ann Arbor: University of Michigan Press, 1999) (http:// www.vpcomm.umich.edu/admissions/research/expert/gurintoc .html); Patricia Gurin, Biren Nagda, and Ximena Zúñiga, *Dialogue across Difference: Practice, Theory, and Research on Intergroup Dialogue* (New York: Russell Sage Foundation, 2013).

8. N. Denson and M. J. Chang, "Dynamic Relationships: Identifying Moderators That Maximize Benefits Associated with Diversity," *Journal of Higher Education* 86, no. 1 (2015): 1–37.

9. Anthony Lising Antonio, Mitchell J. Chang, Kenji Hakuta, David A. Kenny, Shana Levin, and Jeffrey F. Milem, "Effects of Racial Diversity on Complex Thinking in College Students," *Psychological Science* 15, no. 8 (2004): 507–510 (doi:10.1111/j.0956-7976.2004.00710.x).

10. Thomas F. Pettigrew and Linda R. Tropp, *When Groups Meet: The Dynamics of Intergroup Contact* (New York: Psychology Press, 2011); Natalie J. Shook and Russell H. Fazio, "Roommate Relationships: A Comparison of Interracial and Same-Race Living Situations,"

Group Processes and Intergroup Relations 11, no. 4 (2009): 425–437 (doi:10.1177/1368430208095398); Jim Sidanius, Shana Levin, Colette van Laar, and David O. Sears, *The Diversity Challenge: Social Identity and Intergroup Relations on the College Campus* (New York: Russell Sage Foundation, 2008).

11. Shook and Fazio, "Roommate Relationships"; Sidanius et al., *The Diversity Challenge*.

12. Johanne Boisjoly, Greg J. Duncan, Michael Kremer, Dan M. Levy, and Jacque Eccles, "Empathy or Antipathy? The Impact of Diversity," *American Economic Review* 96, no. 5 (2006): 1890.

13. Tamara Towles-Schwen and Russell H. Fazio, "Automatically Activated Racial Attitudes as Predictors of the Success of Interracial Roommate Relationships," *Journal of Experimental Social Psychology* 42, no. 5 (2006): 698–705 (doi:10.1016/j.jesp.2005.11.003); R. E. Phelps, D. B. Altschul, J. M. Wisenbaker, J. F. Day, D. Cooper, and C. G. Potter, "Roommate Satisfaction and Ethnic Identity in Mixed-Race and White University Roommate Dyads," *Journal of College Student Development* 39 (1998): 194–203.

14. Thomas E. Trail, Nicole J. Shelton, and Tessa V. West, "Interracial Roommate Relationships: Negotiating Daily Interactions," *Personality and Social Psychology Bulletin* 35, no. 6 (2009): 671–684 (doi: 10.1177/0146167209332741).

15. Jim Blascovich, Wendy Berry Mendes, Sarah B. Hunter, Brian Lickel, and Neneh Kowai-Bell, "Perceiver Threat in Social Interactions with Stigmatized Others," *Journal of Personality and Social Psychology* 80, no. 2 (2001): 253–267 (doi:10.1037/0022-3514.80.2.253); Walter G. Stephan and Cookie White Stephan, "Intergroup Anxiety," *Journal of Social Issues* 41, no. 3 (1985): 157–175 (doi:10.1111/j.1540-4560.1985.tb01134.x).

16. Pettigrew and Tropp, *When Groups Meet*; Negin R. Toosi, Laura G. Babbitt, Nalini Ambady, and Samuel R. Sommers, "Dyadic Interracial Interactions: A Meta-Analysis," *Psychological Bulletin* 138, no. 1 (2012): 1–27 (doi:10.1037/a0025767).

17. S. C. Wright, "The Next Generation of Collective Action Research," *Journal of Social Issues* 65, no. 4 (2009): 859–879; Sylvia Hurtado, "The Next Generation of Diversity and Intergroup Relations Research," *Journal of Social Issues* 61, no. 3 (2005): 595–610 (doi: 10.1111/j.1540-4560.2005.00422.x).

18. Stéphanie Demoulin, Jacques-Phillippe Leyens, and John F. Dovidio, *Intergroup Misunderstandings: Impact of Divergent Social Realities* (New York: Psychology Press, 2009).

19. Tamar Saguy, John F. Dovidio, and Felicia Pratto, "Beyond Contact: Intergroup Contact in the Context of Power Relations," *Personality and Social Psychology Bulletin* 34, no. 3 (2008): 432–445 (doi:10.1177/0146167207311200).

20. Hilary B. Bergsieker, Nicole J. Shelton, and Jennifer A. Richeson, "To Be Liked versus Respected: Divergent Goals in Interracial Interactions," *Journal of Personality and Social Psychology* 99, no. 2 (2010): 248–264 (doi:10.1037/a0018474).

21. Lawrence D. Bobo, "Somewhere between Jim Crow and Post-Racialism: Reflections on the Racial Divide in America Today," *Daedalus* 140, no. 2 (2011): 11–36 (doi:10.1162/DAED_a_00091).

22. Jennifer A. Richeson and Sophie Trawalter, "Why Do Interracial Interactions Impair Executive Function? A Resource Depletion Account," *Journal of Personality and Social Psychology* 88, no. 6 (2005): 934–947 (doi:10.1037/0022-3514.88.6.934).

23. John Dixon, Linda R. Tropp, Kevin Durrheim, and Colin Tredoux, "'Let Them Eat Harmony': Prejudice-Reduction Strategies and Attitudes of Historically Disadvantaged Groups," *Current Directions in Psychological Science* 19, no. 2 (2010): 76–80 (doi:10.1177/0963721410363366); Ifat Maoz, "Does Contact Work in Protracted Asymmetrical Conflict? Appraising 20 Years of Reconciliation-Aimed Encounters between Israeli Jews and Palestinians," *Journal of Peace Research* 48, no. 1 (2011): 115–125 (doi:10.1177/002 2343310389506).

24. For discussion of structures and processes that produce unequal contributions of more and less privileged people in cross-group communication, see Iris Marion Young, *Intersecting Voices: Dilemmas of Gender, Political Philosophy, and Policy* (Princeton, NJ: Princeton University Press, 1997). Also see the conditions for increasing the likelihood that intergroup contact will produce positive outcomes delineated decades ago by Gordon W. Allport in *The Nature of Prejudice* (Cambridge, MA: Addison-Wesley, 1954).

25. See Elizabeth Cohen's classic work on diverse work groups in elementary school classrooms, Elizabeth G. Cohen and Rachel A. Lotan, *Working for Equity in Heterogeneous Classrooms: Sociological Theory in Practice*, Sociology of Education Series (New York: Teachers College Press, 1997); and recent studies of dynamics in engineering groups and teams, which show, for example, that gender in particular plays a significant role in group work.

26. Lorelle Meadows and Denise Sekaquaptewa, "The Effect of Group Gender Composition on Student Participation and Learning in

Undergraduate Engineering Project Teams," *Proceedings of ASEE Annual Conference*, Vancouver, BC (2011), paper 2011-1319.

27. Roger B. Fisher and Barry N. Checkoway, "Intergroup Dialogue Facilitation for Youth Empowerment and Community Change," in *Facilitating Intergroup Dialogues: Bridging Differences, Catalyzing Change*, ed. Kelly E. Maxwell, Biren (Ratnesh) A. Nagda, and Monita C. Thompson (Sterling, VA: Stylus, 2011); Adriana Aldana, "Youth Civic Engagement: Sociopolitical Development in Schools with Lessons from and for Multicultural Education" (doctoral dissertation, University of Michigan, 2014).

28. For an extended discussion of the pedagogy and theoretical framework guiding intergroup dialogue, as well as a research project assessing its effects, see Gurin, Nagda, and Zúñiga, *Dialogue across Difference*.

29. Ibid.

30. For "bridging" mechanisms that emerge in university/community partnerships jointly engaged in public scholarship that utilizes the diverse talent pool in our nation's metropolitan areas, see Nancy Cantor, "A Map of Opportunity: Anchor Institutions and the Diverse Next Generation" (lecture, University of Southern California Enrollment Center: The Nexus of Mission, Excellence, and Diversity, Los Angeles, January 15, 2014).

31. Kwame A. Appiah, "The Case for Contamination: No to Purity. No to Tribalism. No to Cultural Protectionism. Toward a New Cosmopolitanism," *New York Times Magazine*, January 1, 2006, pp. 30–37, 52 (http://www.nytimes.com/2006/01/01/magazine/01cosmopolitan.html); Martha C. Nussbaum, "Patriotism and Cosmopolitanism," in *For Love of Country: Debating the Limits of Patriotism*, ed. Joshua Cohen (Boston: Beacon Press, 1996); Association of American Colleges and Universities, *College Learning for the New Global Century* (Washington, DC: Association of American Colleges and Universities, National Leadership Council for Liberal Education and America's Promise, 2007) (http://www.aacu.org/advocacy/leap/documents/globalcentury_final.pdf); Partnership for 21st Century Skills, *21st Century Skills, Education and Competitiveness: A Resource and Policy Guide* (Tucson: Partnership for 21st Century Skills, 2008) (http://www.p21.org/storage/documents/21st_century_skills_education_and_competitiveness_guide.pdf).

Chapter 7: Diversity as a Strategic Advantage

1. Marta Tienda, "Demography and the Social Contract," *Demography* 39, no. 4 (2002): 587–616; Kenneth Prewitt, "Beyond Census 2000: As a Nation, We Are the World," *Carnegie Reporter* 1, no. 3 2001): 3–11.

2. Prewitt, "Beyond Census 2000," p. 4.

3. Grutter v. Bollinger, 539 U.S. 306 (2003).

4. Daniel T. Lichter, "Integration or Fragmentation? Racial Diversity and the American Future," *Demography* 50, no. 2 (2013): 359–391.

5. Marta Tienda, "Immigration, Opportunity and Social Cohesion," in *Diversity and Its Discontents: Cultural Conflict and Common Ground in Contemporary American Society*, ed. N. J. Smelser and J. C. Alexander (Princeton, NJ: Princeton University Press, 1999).

6. Ibid., p. 129.

7. Frank Levy, *The New Dollars and Dreams: American Incomes and Economic Change* (New York: Russell Sage Foundation, 1999); Tienda, "Demography and the Social Contract."

8. http://www.ncsl.org/research/immigration/in-state-tuition-and -unauthorized-immigrants.aspx.

9. University of California Regents v. Bakke, 438 U.S. 265 (1978).

10. Lichter, "Integration or Fragmentation?"; Marta Tienda and Norma Fuentes, "Hispanics in Metropolitan America: New Realities and Old Debates," *Annual Review of Sociology* 40 (2014): 499–520; Richard V. Reeves, "The Measure of a Nation," *Annals of the American Academy of Political and Social Science* 657, no. 1 (2015): 22–26.

11. Richard V. Reeves, "Saving Horatio Alger—Equality, Opportunity, and the American Dream," *The Brookings Essay* (2014).

12. Ibid.

13. Lichter, "Integration or Fragmentation?"

14. Samuel H. Preston, "Children and the Elderly: Divergent Paths for America's Dependents," *Demography* 21, no. 4 (1984): 435–457.

15. U.S. Census Bureau, "Poverty Rates by Age: 1959–2009," in *Current Population Survey*, 1960–2010, Annual Social and Economic Supplements (http://www2.census.gov/library/publications/2010/demo /p60–238/pov09fig05.pdf).

16. Julia Isaacs, Katherine Toran, Heather Hahn, Karina Fortuny, and C. E. Steuerle, *Kids' Share 2012: Report on Federal Expenditures on Children through 2011* (Washington DC: Urban Institute, 2012).

17. Michael Leachman and Chris Mai, "Most States Funding Schools Less Than before the Recession" (Center on Budget and Policy

Priorities, May 20, 2014) (http://www.cbpp.org/research/most-states-funding-schools-less-than-before-the-recession).

18. Henry J. Kaiser Family Foundation, "Health Care Costs: A Primer" (Henry J. Kaiser Family Foundation, 2012) (http://kff.org/health-costs/issue-brief/health-care-costs-a-primer/). The Kaiser Family Foundation reports for 2012 that per-person spending on health care averaged $9,744 for seniors (ages 65 and older) compared with $2,500 and $1,700, respectively, for youth ages 0–4 and 5–17.

19. Isaacs et al., *Kids' Share 2012*, figure 9.

20. Center on Budget and Policy Priorities, "Policy Basics: Where Do Our Federal Tax Dollars Go?" (March 11, 2015) (http://www.cbpp.org/cms/?fa=view&id=1258); Jennifer M. Ortman, Victoria A. Velkoff, and Howard Hogan, *An Aging Nation: The Older Population in the United States* (Washington DC: United States Census Bureau, 2014).

21. Isaacs et al., *Kids' Share 2012*.

22. Preston, "Children and the Elderly."

23. The organization was formerly the American Association of Retired Persons but has changed its name to AARP, partly because its membership is not restricted to retirees, as is evident in the lower age threshold for membership.

24. This is starkly evident in Judge Powell's opinion in San Antonio ISD v. Rodriguez, U.S. 1 (1973).

25. See also Lichter, "Integration or Fragmentation?"

26. See http://databank.worldbank.org/data/download/GDP.pdf.

27. James N. Gribble and Jason Bremner, "Achieving a Demographic Dividend," *Population Bulletin* 67, no. 2 (2012): 2–12.

28. Patricia J. Gumport, Maria Iannozzi, Susan Shaman, and Robert Zemsky, "Trends in United States Higher Education from Massification to Post Massification" (Stanford University, National Center for Postsecondary Improvement, 1997).

29. Michael W. Cox and Richard Alm, "Taking Stock in America: Resiliency, Redundancy, and Recovery in the U.S. Economy" (Annual Report of the Federal Reserve Bank of Dallas, 2001) (http://www.dallasfed.org/assets/documents/fed/annual/2001/ar01.pdf).

30. Source: http://www.uis.unesco.org/Pages/default.aspx, accessed March 25, 2015.

31. Robert J. Gordon, "The Great Stagnation of American Education," *New York Times*, September 7, 2013.

32. Organization for Economic Cooperation and Development, "United States," in *Education at a Glance 2013: OECD Indicators* (OECD

Publishing, 2013) (http://www.oecd.org/edu/cag2013%20(eng)--FINAL%2020%20June%202013.pdf).

33. Ibid.

34. Marta Tienda and Faith Mitchell, eds. *Multiple Origins, Uncertain Destinies: Hispanics and the American Future* (Washington, DC: National Academy Press, 2006).

35. National Research Council, *Allocating Federal Funds for Science and Technology: Committee on Criteria for Federal Support of Research and Development* (Washington, DC: National Academy Press, 1995).

36. Because the nonwhite population includes Asians (5 percent of the total), the educational contrasts with whites are less extreme than if they were based on blacks and Hispanics only.

37. National Center for Education Statistics, *Projections of Education Statistics to 2022* (2014) (https://nces.ed.gov/pubs2014/2014051.pdf), table 3, "Actual and Projected Numbers for Enrollment in Public Elementary and Secondary Schools, by Race/Ethnicity: Fall 1997 through Fall 2022."

Index

Italicized pages refer to figures and tables.

OUR COMPELLING INTERESTS

Thomas J. Sugrue, Professor of Social and Cultural Analysis and History, New York University

Beverly Daniel Tatum, President Emerita, Spelman College

Marta Tienda, Maurice P. During '22 Professor, Demographic Studies, and Professor, Sociology and Public Affairs, Princeton University

Sarah E. Turner, Chair, Department of Economics, University of Virginia

Internal Advisory Board

Saleem Badat, Program Director, The Andrew W. Mellon Foundation

Armando I. Bengochea, Program Officer, The Andrew W. Mellon Foundation

Nancy Cantor, Co-chair, Chancellor, Rutgers University-Newark

Makeba Morgan Hill, Deputy to the President and Chief Planner, The Andrew W. Mellon Foundation

Cristle Collins Judd, Senior Program Officer, The Andrew W. Mellon Foundation

Earl Lewis, Co-chair, President, The Andrew W. Mellon Foundation

Doreen N. Tinajero, Program Associate, The Andrew W. Mellon Foundation

Eugene M. Tobin, Senior Program Officer, The Andrew W. Mellon Foundation

Michele S. Warman, Vice President, General Counsel and Secretary, The Andrew W. Mellon Foundation

Laura Washington, Director of Communications, The Andrew W. Mellon Foundation

Mariët Westermann, Vice President, The Andrew W. Mellon Foundation